Gain Confidence

A Guide to Overcoming Fear, Shyness and Low Confidence

Christine Portman

Copyright © Portman Publishing

All rights reserved.
No part of this publication may be reproduced, distributed, or transmitted in any form or by any means, including photocopying, recording, or other electronic or mechanical methods, without the prior written permission of the publisher, except in the case of brief quotations embodied in critical reviews and certain other non-commercial uses permitted by copyright law.

Table of Contents

Gain Confidence & Self-Esteem..........1

Part I: When Confidence and Courage Fail.......................7
It's Time For A Restart In Life...7
Self-esteem, Confidence & Courage 13
Case Study: Leslie's Limiting Beliefs 15
Case Study: It's Only Joe 16
Case Study: Workplace Wendy 18
You need both courage and confidence in your life........21
Your Confidence/Courage Inventory...............................22
Self-Esteem Challenges…and How To Overcome Them ..26
The Need For Validation 27
Getting Your Basic Needs Met 30

Your Master Brain 34
Gender, Culture and Self-Esteem 39
The 4 Dimensions and Your Role in Each One Begin with the Blueprint 47
The Quality of Life you Deserve 57
Not What You Might Expect 69
Convenience vs. Courage 73
How To Gain Experience and Lose Your Fear..................76
The PSP Circle 79

Do more than live – thrive!..*84*

How To Stop Giving Up..*86*

Developing Courage and Confidence *89*

6 Acts of Courage *93*

How To Easily Harness The Power Of Your Mind..........*104*

The One Question You Must Ask Yourself *111*

Taking Action Now *119*

Confident body language and dress..............................*119*

*Courage Hacks: The Secret Habits of Confident People**126*

Going Forward In Life *129*

How To Overcome Anxiety & Worry Through Mindfulness. Deal with worry, stress, panic, fear & negative thinking. 131

Beating Anxiety and Worry *132*

PART 1: BEATING ANXIETY & STRESS *136*

The Defining Terms..*137*

Real Life Case Study: Serena *143*

Chapter 1 Takeaways *145*

Chapter 2 - The Stress of Relationships *147*

The Most Important Relationship In Your Life 147
Relationships With Partners 150
Your Relationship With Your Kids 154
The Relationship With Family and Friends 157
Chapter 2 Take-Aways... 159

Chapter 3 - Creating Your Future 161
Dealing With Your Issues 164
Sorting Through Your Anxiety Triggers 168
Real Life Case Study:.. 169
Chapter 3 Takeaways 172

PART 2: STRATEGIES FOR SUCCESS............................ 174
Chapter 4 - Creating Space and Making Changes......... 175
Clearing Clutter from Your Physical Space 178
Clearing Clutter from Your Mental Space..................... 181
Chapter 4 Takeaways 186

Chapter 5 Mindfulness – This Changes Everything 188
Simple Techniques for Everyday Mindfulness............... 190
A Key Principle To Change 194
A Positive Change.. 195
A Helping Hand On Your Journey 196
De-Stressing 198

Chapter 5 Takeaways *199*

Chapter 6 – The Power of "Fun" *201*
A Daily Dose of Laughter *202*
How To Share the Fun *205*
In Praise of Praise *206*
The Key To "Play" *207*
Real Life Case Study *208*
Chapter 6 Take-aways *210*

Chapter 7 – How To Look After Your Body *211*
Tuning In *212*
Do This! This Can Change A Lot! *215*
Breathing: This Is How You Should Do It To Reduce Anxiety *219*
Getting Better Sleep! *220*
Looking After Yourself *222*
Chapter 7 Takeaways *223*

Chapter 8 – Easily Harnessing The Power of your Mind *225*
You Are What You Think *227*
Taking Control *229*
The Steps To Reframing Your Thoughts *234*
Chapter 8 Takeaways *236*

Chapter 9 - Creativity Is Key *238*

Creativity Easily Explained *239*
Some Easy Ways To Be More Creative *240*
This Can Really Reduce Your Anxiety & Stress *242*
The Time For Change *244*
An Added Bonus *245*
Real Life Case Study *247*
Chapter 9 Take-aways *248*

Chapter 10 - Handing Things Over *250*
It Can Help, If You Let It *252*
Deciding What You Need *252*
Exploring Alternatives *254*
Asking for Help *255*
Chapter 10 Takeaways *256*

Conclusion: Starting Again *258*

Thank you so much for checking out my book. *260*

Part I: When Confidence and Courage Fail

It's Time For A Restart In Life

Have you ever noticed how some people have tons of confidence? Nothing bothers them. They don't let anything get in their way. Regardless of how volatile the situation or new the experience, confident people take it in stride. It seems like they're able to tackle just about anything, whether they have any prior experience in the matter or not.

Their cup of confidence is full, and it often runs over.

Those who are confident and courageous are more afraid of having never tried anything and missing out than trying something and failing.

Move across the county to take on a new job? Why not?
Swim with sharks? Sure.
Face down a sneering bully? Easy!
People with self-esteem and confidence have no fear.

Not everyone has confidence in such spades. Other people have convinced themselves they can't commit to an action before they even get started. They can't have a conversation with a stranger. They can try something new, even though it sounds like it could be fun. They can't stand up for themselves – or for anyone else. Their confidence is in limited supply, and that tamps down their courage. You've probably witnessed, or experienced, this lack of courage and confidence in action.

Imagine a scene like this: **The Neighbor**

You bought a new house, and you're especially proud of the place you call home. It's not the Taj Mahal, but it's nice enough for you and your family, and it even has a green space. You're no green thumb, but you've been looking forward to having an area where the kids could play ball. Perhaps you could plant a few vegetables, maybe even some flowers, and you'd have a righteous little garden.

Then a new neighbor moves in next door. Her property is smaller than yours, and although it's situated oddly on her lot, you always thought the little cottage looked quaint. Your neighbor doesn't feel the same way. She knocks on your door to demand that you remove your fence immediately because it's in her way, and she won't have it blocking her view.

As much as you try to explain that your fence is built inside your lot line, your neighbor will have none of that. Her next step is to hire a surveyor to assess where the property line actually lies.

The survey results come back. Your fence is indeed on your property.

"Well I just don't have room to do everything I want to do on my property," says the neighbor. *"I need more space. And it's not like you're doing anything with yours."*

Before you know it, she has begun planting assorted shrubs on your property where the two lots butt up against each other. She's also dug a culvert across the front of your lawn to divert the water away from her home when it rains.

"After all, all you have growing there are weeds," she spits when you try to say something about it. *"It's not like I'm hurting anything."*

She's probably right. She isn't hurting anything, but she's encroaching on your piece of property. Your little piece of heaven. She's a bully.

Maybe you're thinking, I would march right over there, give her a large piece of my mind, and tell her to get her shrubs out of my yard. After all, It's my yard, not hers. What gives her the right to take over my yard? Or possibly, you'd go a step further by pulling out the shrubs by their roots and dumping the mess on her doorstep. Either way, you'd put a stop to her nonsense. If you agree that confronting your neighbor about her actions is the right thing to do, congratulations. You are in the minority.

Not many people would talk to their neighbor about her behavior. They would let the problem fester until it becomes uglier than it already is. That's because most people don't want any trouble. They prefer not to speak up, even when they are in the right. Instead, they look the other way, hoping the problem will solve itself, but of course, it never does. And besides, what if it turns out that you're being the difficult one? Is it really such a bad thing to let your neighbor use part of your yard, even though you had other plans for it?

"I don't want to disturb the peace," you think. *"I just don't want any problems with my neighbors."*

In reality, your neighbor has already disturbed your peace, and her behavior is definitely a problem. How much more conflict and anxiety are you willing to endure? There are a lot of good reasons for avoiding confrontation. Maybe you're worried that your neighbor won't like you if you stand up for yourself, and all the other neighbors on your street will hate you, too. You might be concerned about hurting your neighbor's feelings. What if she thinks you're impossible to be around?

The fear of separation can be a legitimate concern. We humans are at our best when we're part of a well-functioning group or community. Our safety and well-being depends on our ability to get along with others. That's why many people keep their emotions bottled up within. They don't want their social and professional circles to know what they really feel or think. They are gaslighters.

Gaslighters tend to hold back these pent-up emotions until they reach the breaking point. Then their true feelings burst, spewing angry words everywhere, leaving everyone in the vicinity wondering where that came from. If you know that you are prone to gaslighting tendencies like this, you may hesitate to speak up for yourself.

Other people avoid confrontation altogether because they second-guess their own opinions and knowledge. They're not sure of themselves. Their self-esteem is low. They have little to no faith that they are competent enough to take care of the problem or embark on a new path. What if they fail? Let's look back at that scenario with your neighbor.

You begin thinking, maybe it's unreasonable to expect your neighbor to keep her plants in her own yard. After all, she sent you a text saying all of the neighbors agreed with her that you are being contrary. You assume she's right; the other neighbors must hate you. You even assume that maybe your plants won't look as good as hers, anyway. Soon, these assumptions will sap your confidence. Without confidence, your self-esteem begins to sag.

Then you talk yourself into giving up altogether. You're no longer interested in developing the confidence you need, because what does it matter? One more conversation with your neighbor won't change a thing. The assumptions you've been making are now limiting your beliefs and your actions. These limiting beliefs act as an anchor, weighing you down, and preventing you from developing confidence and having courage. You lack the confidence to confront a wrong and make it right. You're in the right, but you won't stand up for yourself because you're afraid that you may be isolating yourself. You are afraid to speak up for yourself because you can only imagine what might happen.

Interestingly, no one is born with this hesitation. We develop legitimate and rational fears throughout our lifetimes, and they exist to protect us from harm.

Humans have only two fears at birth: the fear of loud noises, and the fear of falling. We are programmed with these innate fears as a way to keep us safe. Loud noises indicate the possibility of danger nearby. Falling can be equally dangerous because we could be injured. These fears – the fear of loud noises and the fear of falling -- keep us safe. But what about everything else we're afraid of, like public speaking, animals with beady eyes, and crazy neighbors? Everything else we fear is a learned behavior. There's a good reason for some of our learned fears. They also keep us safe.

Arachnophobia, the fear of spiders, is a real fear for many people. In fact, up to 40% of our phobias have something to do with rodents, snakes or crawly things, like spiders and scorpions. We learn spider-phobias. No one is born with arachnophobia. Babies are not innately afraid of spiders. Somewhere along the way, humans had a frightful experience with an audacious spider or scorpion. Anyone who has been stung by a scorpion knows all too well how the pain can be seared in your memory for a long time. The experience creates an intense emotion, and that emotion now triggers fear any time you see an arachnid. The fear of spiders (and scorpions) keeps us safe.

It's a protective mechanism, and we develop a lot of these protective responses through our lives.

For example, people have discovered that stoves are hot and can start a fire. We learn that pointed objects pierce the skin and cause pain. Animals with forward-facing eyes seek out prey for their meals. We become cautious around these animals because we don't like the idea of being prey. Along the way, we've even been made aware that the worst flesh-eating zombies attack at night, turning everyone in their path into an undead creature.

There's a lot we have to learn to be afraid of! We manage to convince ourselves to be afraid of other people, too.

Sometimes, our anthropophobia – the fear of people – is a prudent course of action. Large crowds can be scary, especially if they become rowdy. Other times, however, social anxiety holds us back. We are so concerned about getting judged by those around us that we allow our fear to control our behavior.

How many people do you know who are afraid to even talk to someone, especially if there is the slightest chance the other person might disagree? It's likely that they are suffering from two fears: the fear of disagreeing with another person, and the fear of stating an opinion. Both concerns are learned behaviors. At one time, we might have been completely assured of ourselves, unafraid to step out and speak our minds. Or try something new. Our confidence levels were high because we believed in our ability to make something happen. We expected no less than a positive outcome. What happened to our confidence?

Something happened that made us doubt ourselves. If a traumatic event occurred, we lost our confidence immediately. Small disappointments can have negative effects as well. Eventually, the culmination of each setback stole our willingness to try again. Every ounce of self-esteem evaporated, leaving us to face our fears, and suddenly, we no longer have any courage, either.

Self-esteem, Confidence & Courage

Confidence and self-esteem go hand-in-hand with each other. It's hard to have one without the other, and you need them both if you're going to have the kind of courage you need to get through life. Self-esteem is the belief that you deserve respect. You have a sense that you have value and are worthy. You are worthy of all things related to having a good life: eating, sleeping, playing, learning, and loving are just a few of the areas in your life. Because of this value, you will not let others hurt you physically, emotionally, intellectually, or spiritually. You won't treat yourself that way, either.

Let's take a look at confidence next. In its simplest terms, confidence is the degree to which you believe in yourself and know that you will succeed. When your self-esteem is high, you can accept who you are as a person. You're okay with what you look like, the level of skills that you have, and how you act. Your confidence is high, and as a result, you fell courageous, too.

Lose your self-esteem, and you won't have much confidence. A lack of confidence can squash your courage.

Your courage comes from you knowing that the outcome will be positive regardless of whatever you do. Even if you take on the scariest thing you can think of, your courage will get you through it. Your confidence and your self-esteem back up that feeling. Can you have one without the other? The answer is yes, but the result is rarely positive.

People with low self-esteem and high levels of confidence are willing to take excessive risks without regard to the outcome, no matter how negative it might be. They come across as know-it-alls, arrogant fools who have a high opinion of themselves. These people may even place themselves in dangerous situations, accept one-way missions, and be willing to lose everything. For them, it's often all or nothing. There is no compromise.

What about those with high self-esteem and low confidence? They accept themselves for who they are, but their lack of confidence prevents them from expressing themselves around peers and co-workers. The person with high self-esteem and low confidence can speak passionately about subjects with which they are familiar, especially if discussing them one-to-one or in small groups. Having to speak to a larger group doesn't reduce their self-esteem. They hesitate to speak up because they are not confident.

Those with low self-esteem and low confidence are often victims who perceive that the world happens to them rather than having any control over events in their lives. High self-esteem almost *always* results in confidence. When either self-esteem or confidence are missing from your life, you are less likely to realize your full potential. You narrow the possibilities in front of you. You accept far less than you deserve. You fail to live abundantly.

Let's look at three stories of people who lacked self-esteem, confidence, or both.

Case Study: Leslie's Limiting Beliefs

Leslie was a smart young woman. She excelled in school, particularly in mathematics and science, and she took advanced classes at every opportunity. She secretly hoped to go to the university and then to medical school, where she could study to be a doctor. Leslie's dad, on the other hand, did not want her going off to college.

"You'll just end up getting pregnant and maybe getting married," he said. *"Any money your mom and I have would be ill-spent on your education. You going off to some university would be like throwing our good, hard-earned money down the drain. You'll just waste every bit of it by taking endless classes, never graduating, and never being a doctor."*

Leslie figured that this was her dad's way of saying her parents couldn't afford to send her to college. She was so determined to find a way to make her dreams come true that she worked even harder in school. When Leslie was offered a full-ride scholarship for the first four years of school, she proudly showed the scholarship to her father.

"That's nice, but you can't go," he said. *"Women don't need to go to medical school, and they don't need to become doctors. Why don't you just get married and have kids? That's all you're destined to do, anyway."*

Immensely hurt by her father's words, that's exactly what Leslie did. On the day she turned 18, she agreed to marry her boyfriend. They had a small and understated wedding ceremony, and within a year, Leslie had their first child. Medical school became nothing more than a faraway dream because she put all of her focus on raising her children. She denied herself the opportunity to change her circumstances and those of the patients she might have treated.

The sad thing is that there are Leslie's all over the world. Young women are held back because they accepted the limiting beliefs and assumptions of someone in their family. Leslie has low self-esteem and high levels of confidence. She believed her father's assumptions as though they were her own. Rather than find a way to go to university and med school, Leslie gave in. She immediately jumped into a marriage and child-rearing without even considering a compromise.

In doing so, Leslie lost her self-esteem but maintained her focus by concentrating on her children instead of her studies. But what happens when the levels of self-esteem and confidence are reversed?

Case Study: It's Only Joe

Joe is the opposite of Leslie. He has high levels of self-esteem and low confidence levels. Here's how they manifest themselves in his life:

Joe is a great guy. He's likeable, and he has a lot of friends. They're a good group, equally likeable, and they're fun to hang out with.

Joe enjoys their company, whether they decide to play a few rounds of golf or drink a few rounds at the local pub. They always have a good time, and Joe appreciates feeling like he's part of the gang.

Sooner or later though, the guys in the group start talking about sports and then politics. They begin to get rowdy, and their language gets just as colorful and loud. Then the guys make rude comments about the women they know. Sometimes they even talk about the women sitting within earshot at nearby tables.

Occasionally, they notice that Joe looks away of stares into his drink when they do this.

"Aw, it's only Joe," they say, and they continue on in merriment.

Joe wants desperately to be one of the guys, but he also finds it extremely uncomfortable when they become boisterous or decide what they're going to do for entertainment without even asking Joe – as though he doesn't even have an opinion! Joe doesn't always agree with their political viewpoints either, and he especially does not like to listen to the ugly things they say about women. But the problem is that Joe won't speak up. He's afraid to say what he really thinks. He worries that if he does, his friends might not like him anymore. They might not invite him to hang around with them. And then where would he be? At home, alone, that's where.

What about Joe's friends? They have no idea that he feels the way he does. The problem is that Joe lacks the courage of his convictions. As much as he knows the right thing to do, He's afraid to step up and do it. And He's worried about what everyone else thinks rather than being worried about doing the right thing. Joe has high self-esteem and low confidence.

Like Leslie, Joe lets other people's assumptions hold him. He cannot be true to himself because he's trying to fit in with everyone else.

Case Study: Workplace Wendy

It's even harder for people with low self-esteem and low confidence. Their courage is non-existent, as we see in the next story:

It had been a tough job market, with good jobs being few and far between. Finding the right job was even harder. Wendy's husband had been laid off work after injuring his leg, and he was not working at all – nor could he work for at least a year, the doctor had said.

He didn't even have an income; their ability to pay the bills and put food on the table lay squarely on Wendy's shoulders. They had already run through their meager savings, so now she had to find a job.

Wendy should have been ecstatic about going to work for Murphy & Associates when they asked her to join their team. She would be able to earn good money now and maybe even get a little ahead. When he interviewed her, the owner suggested there was the potential to more than double her salary if she stayed with the company.

"It's an opportunity I 'm going to have to take," she told her husband. *"This position may be an entry level job now,*

but there's so much more opportunity ahead for me – for us, if I can work my way up. I can't say no."

Wendy's husband expressed his concern about the job's hourly requirements. Wendy might have to work some pretty long hours every once in a while. By the time she caught one of the late buses home, it could be nine or ten at night.

"Don't worry," Wendy reassured her husband. *"I'll have dinner ready for you to microwave on those nights. You can have your supper, and I'll eat when I get in. It won't be often."*

In the back of her mind, she tried telling herself that the hours wouldn't be a problem. If they were, she'd say something.

Her husband was less worried about his supper than he was about her safety. Call him old-fashioned, but he didn't like the idea of Wendy being at work so late and traveling home alone. At first, Wendy had to work late one or two nights at the end of each month. She could see why. The long days took place right before the monthly billing cycle, and preparing customer invoices took a while. By the time Wendy had worked with Murphy & Associates for a quarter of the year, she had to stay late every night of the week. She couldn't say no. After all, she was the most recent hire, the lowest in rank in the office, so of course the duties fell to her.

Her husband pointed out that these practices didn't seem like an efficient way to run a business, but Wendy insisted, with tears in her eyes, that she needed to work the hours, or her boss would fire her. And she needed the job. They needed the job. It's how her life was going to be, probably forever. She felt trapped.

By the time the second quarter rolled around, Wendy was exhausted. She hadn't been getting enough sleep. She woke up early every morning to catch the bus to work, and she returned late at night. By the time she got home, she was too tired to eat, so she showered and tumbled into bed. In a few hours the cycle started all over again.

"How nice that you get plenty of sleep," she snapped at her husband.

In six months' time, Wendy lost weight, looked gaunt, and she was sporting a big pair of *"panda eyes."* The dark circles under her eyes told the story of her lack of sleep and progressively worsening health.

"It's your fault that I look like this," Wendy said. *"If you could do anything to help around the house, my life would be a lot easier. It's just not fair."*

What Wendy didn't tell her husband was that the boss had given her a choice about staying late to work on projects.

"If you don't have anything pressing," said Mr. Murphy, *"I have some extra files I'd like a second pair of eyes on. You have a knack for details, and if you can make the time, that would be great. Of course, I'll understand if this job isn't important enough to you to make the commitment. I guess that's why I'm always looking for the right person, someone who wants to treat this like a career."*

Wendy held back another sigh. Why did bosses always pick on her? It was just
her luck.

"Oh course, I'll take care of it," she said. She couldn't even force her mouth into a smile anymore. Her life was a wreck, for sure.

Unable and unwilling to speak up for herself, Wendy had low self-esteem and low confidence. Everything in life – hers and her husband's -- happened to her. She had no mastery over anything. She was a victim, and she couldn't figure out how to regain control of her self-esteem, her confidence, or even her life.

Had she had any confidence in her ability to speak up for herself, Wendy may have handled the requests for working overtime quite differently. She may even have seen the situation for what it was – an opportunity.

Unfortunately, those who feel victimized have little ability to hold clarifying conversations that establish expectations. Wendy's story is not that much different from the story about the neighborhood bully.

You need both courage *and* confidence in your life

Every scenario in this chapter shows how a lack of self-esteem and confidence can prevent you from achieving your goals and doing well in your life. You may have thought that you picked up a book on self-esteem and confidence, so what do all these scenarios about bullying have to do with courage, confidence, and vulnerability? As it turns out, a lot.

We often allow bullies to take away our self-esteem and confidence, and that leaves us with plenty of self-doubts. We feel like there's nothing we can do about any of the problems, and as a result, we become vulnerable. And we stop there.

Ask yourself these refection questions:

How would each outcome be different if Lisa, Joe, and Wendy had the self-esteem and confidence they needed for what they were doing?

Would that have given them the courage to change their actions? How so?

What would have happened if they have been able to use their vulnerability to change their lives?

That's what this book is about. This book will teach you how to identify the situations causing you to cave in and accept less than you're worth.

You'll discover how assumptions and limiting beliefs are holding you back from developing self-esteem and confidence. Together, we'll explore more of what the self-esteem and confidence connection is and what it isn't, where it comes from, and how to get more of it. You'll also find out how to use your doubts, your anxiety, and especially your vulnerability to forge your courage. We'll even look at how courageous people have inspired others to keep going.

Your Confidence/Courage Inventory

Knowing where you stand and how you would respond in any situation is your key to growing a successful mindset. Before you start the next chapter, identify your own levels of self-esteem and confidence, your strengths and weaknesses. Take a moment to reflect on each of the scenarios presented in this chapter. For each set of questions, focus on the first response that comes to your mind.

If you were Leslie, what would you have done? Would you have accepted your dad's assessment that you had no business attempting university classes and medical school? Does money limit what you can and cannot do? Would you have defied your parent and gone to college anyway?

Have you ever been in a situation similar to Joe's? Has there been a time when you sat by silently, uncomfortable with the conversation, but afraid to speak out against it? Maybe you had an opportunity to express your religious or political views, but kept them to yourself? Or perhaps you were aware that the comments you heard were also making others feel awkward, but you didn't put a stop to them?

Was there ever a time that you felt as though your family, your friends, and the entire world were working against you? That everything that happened was always the wrong thing, and the result of bad luck? Did you feel like everybody was out to get you? That if it weren't for bad luck, you'd have no luck at all?

And finally, how would you have handled the neighborhood bully? Would you have stood up for your rights and put her in her place, or would you let your neighbor continue to take advantage of you and use your property?

For every scenario in which you would have stood up for yourself, give yourself one point. For every scenario where you would have stood up for another person, add two points. However, if you would have given in and given up, subtract one point for each scenario.

Add up your subtotals. What number did you get?

Here's what your self-esteem and confidence score looks like:

If you scored -4 to 0, don't give up! You're working from a position of vulnerability. Unfortunately, that vulnerability is not working for you. Not right now, anyway. Your self-esteem and your confidence both need a boost. The good news is that you are in a position to recreate your worldview and come back stronger than ever.

Did you get 1 to 4 points? Your self-esteem and confidence is there, but you've kept them both hidden. You use them only when absolutely necessary, and the rest of the time you tuck them away. You are cautious in deciding when to be courageous and when to step back from confrontation, but you would benefit from increasing your willingness to step out of your comfort zone.

For those of you who accrued 5 to 8 points, know that you're on your way to growing the confidence and self-esteem that will carry you forward. Neither a victim nor an arrogant person, your self-esteem and made you confident most of the time. You can't rest yet, though, because there are still times that uncertainty looms ahead, suggesting the possibility of your action – or inaction -- derailing you from your tracks.

If you have an earned score of 8 to 12, you're confident in most situations. You'll want to take care, however, that this confidence does not develop into braggadocio. Over-confidence can lead to carelessness, especially in relationships. Others may think of you as self-centered and narcissistic; therefore, you'll have to check in with yourself to make sure your confidence does not become recklessness.

With your self-esteem and confidence score in hand, you're ready to take the first steps in identifying the challenges that the lack of either can bring you. Once you know where your obstacles lie, you can develop strategies that build up your self-esteem and confidence. You'll have the courage you need to take action.

In the chapters ahead, you'll learn how your physical and emotional well-being affect each other, as well as techniques to pinpoint when you must intervene on your own behalf. We'll explore at how a person can elevate his or her self-esteem and increase their confidence in most situations, regardless of gender or background. You'll have a toolbox of techniques you can use to help yourself live courageously.

You don't have to let your self-esteem and confidence fail you. You can develop the courage you need to take action. Let's explore the next steps in building the kind of self-esteem and confidence that will help you live the life you want and deserve.

Self-Esteem Challenges...and How To Overcome Them

We are a network of collaborators. We're meant to be that way. We do our best work when we join efforts with others within a dynamic community to support each other. Most people need to feel as though they can provide value within the community they live and work. For many people, that means for being a part of a neighborhood or functioning within well-defined social circle parameters. Others find significance in the busy and well-integrated hive that makes up their professional world.

People are naturally drawn to join groups with similar interests. You may belong to a group of sports enthusiasts or supportive young mothers. There are groups for people with all kinds of hobbies, conditions, and careers. Even people who profess to having no hobby or outside interests can still find groups with which to connect via social media platforms like *LinkedIn, Instagram,* and *Facebook.*

We want to be accepted.

That's why likes are so popular on social media pages. People in social media communities seek validation from button clicks. Every thumbs-up, heart, and other positive emoji help us build our self-esteem and develop confidence. Every click is a positive affirmation that the events in our lives and what we do about them matter not just to ourselves, but to other people as well. The more likes and loves, the more we feel validated.

The Need For Validation

Validation is, perhaps, one of the greatest things we can do for each other. To validate someone is to acknowledge that their feelings and beliefs have value and are worth holding onto. By validating another person, you are not just confirming a fact; you are also affirming that person's existence. You recognize that another human being has value. We all need that kind of affirmation. Affirmation is what tells us that we are on the right track in this thing called life.

There is not one of us who got an owner's manual when we started our journey as a baby. There has been no checklist handed out to all the participants in life, with neat and tidy boxes to tick off as we accomplish each right of passage. For most of us, life events don't always arrange themselves in a logical order. Things happen, and we do the best we can, wondering if we're even on the right track. Each of us muddles our way through experiences common and unique.

We get some sort of education, make friends, and develop relationships with others. Some of us remain healthy, others get sick, and most of us love at least one other person in our lives. We have friends, develop likes and dislikes, and have opinions about the things that matter most to us. It's the rare individual, however, who doesn't wonder if their existence made a difference in the grand scheme of things. Wouldn't it be nice to know for sure?

That's where validation comes in. Validation is knowing that you have significance and that you make a difference. The things you do and say have value to others, and you're normal for needing validation.

What Validation Is Not

Validation is not a judgment. By validating another person, you are not evaluating whether their actions are good or bad. You are merely acknowledging that they happened. You provide assurance. When you validate another person, you are affirming an experience that most other people have experienced.

Imagine a young mother trying to check out at the grocery, her two tired toddlers having run out of patience and interest Long ago. The line at the cashier has been long, and now the customer trying to pay at the register who had to send someone back to get another item, is digging through her bag to find the extra money for the purchase. Everyone in line rolls their eyes and sighs heavily, exasperated by the additional delay.

The mom with the two little kids becomes mortified when both children let out piercing screams. Their wails seem to pierce the walls. Neither child is in pain; they are simply tired and beyond ready for a nap.

Mom tries to hush them and distract them until she can check out.

"It's okay," says the older man in line behind her. *"We've all been there. Your kids are just being normal kids. It's all going to be okay."*

That simple validation may well be enough for the mom to finish her shopping and get the kids home for their naps. The validation that her kids are like everybody else's kids Is what helps her get through this moment. She's not a bad mom. She's just experiencing something that a lot of others have already been through and survived. Validation is not advice, either. A person who needs validation is not seeking advice, no matter how well intentioned it might be.

When you validate someone, you confirm that others have had similar experiences. You're not alone, and you're not crazy. Remember the story about Leslie and what her father told her about going to university and med school? After her dad dashed her hopes, her disappointment was obvious. Her dreams evaporated into thin air. Leslie faced a future she didn't want, but she felt guilty about not accepting the destiny that had been laid out before her.

She had grown up in a home where validation rarely occurred, if at all. Maybe, she thought, my dad's right. Maybe I don't belong in school. Maybe all I'm good for is being a wife and having children. Leslie needed a friend who could tell her, *"You have every right to feel disappointed. Anyone in your shoes would feel the same way. You can, however, overcome this."*

We need to know that our experiences and the feelings that result from them are not so strange and uncommon that they cannot be overcome. And validation provides the words we need to hear.

Withholding validation can result in isolation. That isolation prevents people from being connected with each other. In the long run, isolation can create lasting negative effects, including uncertainty and depression. Without a connection to others, we are unsure if anything we are experiencing is even normal. Leslie was isolated from a potential career and from being able to work with others who shared a similar passion for taking care of people.

She faced tremendous upheaval in her life. She was going to be kicked out of the only home she knew. She had no idea if she would be safe. The father's decision made her doubt if he even loved her, and that impacted not only her self-esteem, but also her self-actualization.

Leslie was about to experience complete upheaval in her life. Validation helped her understand she is not alone, and that others have gone through similar experiences. All of her thoughts, emotions, and actions were completely normal for a person in her situation. Anyone who had an experience like this would feel the same way! Accepting the validation, however, may be another story altogether. Acceptance comes from taking care of your basic needs.

Getting Your Basic Needs Met

In the last century, psychologist Abraham Maslow developed a theory about human motivation. He devoted his studies to constructing a framework that could describe the varying stages of growth in a human's life, and this framework is still in use today. According to Maslow, every human being has basic needs they seek to take care of.

Imagine each of these needs arranged in a pyramid, with the most basic conditions building the foundation for everything else. Maslow named each of the steps in the hierarchy as follows: Physiological, Safety, Love and Belonging, Esteem, and Self-Actualization. Each level must be satisfied before the next one can be realized, so it makes sense that the levels progress upward.

The first level, the physiological, consists of what you need for survival. All humans need air, water, food, and sleep. The absence of any of these threatens human existence.

However, the person who can we meet these basic physiological needs can then look out for his or her safety. Safety is the next level up in the pyramid.

Safety can mean a lot of things including having shelter and with people who will not harm you. Security can take a lot of different forms including health, emotional, spiritual, and even financial conditions. Having a job may take care of your financial safety needs, but your emotional safety may be at risk if you feel threatened in the workplace, like Wendy. Without safety, a person cannot ascend any higher in the pyramid. If your physiological and safety needs met, your next need is social belonging. This is belonging and love is the community in which you live. Your family, your friends, and even your colleagues make up this social network.

It's at this plateau that the connections we make matter significantly. Humans need to know that they are part of a group, and that together with this group, regardless of its size, every member will work to improve their ability to meet their physiological and safety needs. This is every bit as true for a large professional organization as it is the intimate relationship between two people. The inability or failure to fit in may spell trouble for an individual's safety needs as well as physiological needs. People who are excluded from social belonging experience more isolationism and low self-esteem, and they're less likely to build confidence. As a result, those on the fringe of society are more likely to succumb to peer pressure.

On the other hand, if the need for love and belonging has been met, the individual feels more competent and confident. This person is on their way to building self-esteem, which is the next hierarchy. Esteem comes from recognition, and for many people, that means earning a specific level of status among those in the community. These achievement-oriented people who yearn for respect, but the judgment of others affects their self-esteem.

Remember Joe? He was the friend who loved to hang out with his buddies but never felt confident enough to tell them his opinion, whether that was where he'd like to go eat or why making fun of strangers was inappropriate and how uncomfortable it made him feel.

Joe's need for personal respect was so great that he couldn't insist on respecting others. Respecting others is a much nobler level in the hierarchy, but until Joe gets the respect – or attention -- he seeks, he will be unable to advocate for others, or to reach self-actualization, which is the next level. Like Leslie, Joe may suffer from a loss of self-esteem and even fall into depression. If, however, Joe obtains respect and can advocate for the respect of others, he will be that much closer to self-actualization. He will become the person he's always been capable of being. People who reach the level of self-actualization accomplish the goals they set out to achieve.

Imagine if Leslie went back to school, and earned her degrees. With each certification, she would feel more validated. She would be more assured that she could meet the basic needs of herself and her family. She could provide for their safety, and find supportive groups with which to belong. As a result, she would experience greater self-esteem, and she would reach self-actualization.

Joe's personal trajectory might follow a similar path. As he rose in the triangle through each hierarchy, he would become more self-assured and confident, and he would have the courage to speak up. Ultimately, Joe and Leslie could both reach self-transcendence, which, according to

Maslow, is the final level of human consciousness. Leslie and Joe could become altruistic.

This level may not be possible for Wendy to reach. Having become the family's sole breadwinner, Leslie had an opportunity to master each level of Maslow's hierarchy. Her new job would meet hers and her husband's physiological and physical safety needs, and she would find an expanded network for belonging. In turn, this connectivity could increase her self-esteem and lead to self-actualization. Unfortunately, Wendy took on the role of the victim instead. Rather than seek validation for her actions, she allowed herself to create limiting beliefs and make assumptions that prevented her from growing as a human and achieving her capacity for greatness.

Wendy needed to know that her husband had her back. That he appreciated her stepping in to become the breadwinner. Had he known what to do, Wendy's husband could have validated her in three simple steps: **affirm, acknowledge**, and **accept**.

The validation process would look like this:

AFFIRM: *"Wendy, you are putting in a lot of hours, and I see how hard you are working. I hear you saying that you feel as though you're carrying the load by yourself. Is that right?"*

Affirmation comes from observation. To affirm, state what you see going on. Make your observation as matter-of-factly as possible.

ACKNOWLEDGE: *"It sounds like you are feeling frustrated."*

Notice that this statement is not an accusation; it's an observation. Acknowledge the other person's emotions matter-of-factly.

ACCEPT: *"It's understandable that you feel this way. Taking on this burden can be frustrating/worrisome/overwhelming."*

Show that you understand what she's going through. You hear what's being said. You're not necessarily agreeing. There's no judgment. You are recognizing that she has these feelings, and she's entitled to have them.

What happens after the validation is up to the parties involved. Wendy may end the conversation, but more often than not, the validation opens the door to communication. The validation we receive can be the difference between forging ahead and giving up altogether.

Your Master Brain

It's too bad that you can't validate yourself as easily as you can provide validation for others.

How efficient would it be to tell yourself, *"Self, I appreciate how well you stuck it out on this challenge. You worked hard even though the journey wasn't easy. It would have been a rocky road for anyone to travel. It's understandable that you feel tired!"*

Unfortunately, it usually doesn't work that way. The human brain needs validation, but validating ourselves is hard to do. You have to rely on your own experiences to affirm, acknowledge, and accept your thoughts and feelings. Doing so requires looking at yourself objectively, and that's no easy feat.

It's often a skill that only the most mature and most experienced of us ever master. That mastery depends entirely on our ability to meet – or exceed – the milestones, goals, and standards set before us. Self-esteem comes from meeting those expectations. If you don't have self-esteem, no amount of validating will trick the human brain into thinking its owner is appreciated and valued. That recognition must come from external sources. It's how the brain is wired.

To understand how the brain works, let's create a model for reference. Clench both of your hands into fists. Put your fists together, with the thumbs next to each other and facing you. What you have is a physical representation of your brain.

Look at your brain model from every angle. Your thumbs represent the frontal cortex, which is one of the last areas of the brain to develop completely. At the top of the model, where your folded fingers fit together, knuckle to knuckle, that's your cerebrum. There are various lobes in the cerebrum. Each lobe plays a role in how your body and your mind function as they work together every day at work and every night while you're sleeping. Jointly, the lobes make up the central storage and housing for most of what you do throughout your day.

The cerebrum helps you see, hear, and feel, which in turn, keeps you safe. Your brain is constantly analyzing every element it identifies to determine risk factors for you. That's not the only responsibility of the cerebrum. The lobes in the cerebrum also handle complex thinking processes, like performing mathematical functions or learning a new language. Once again, look at the physical model of the brain you created with your hands.

Your wrists form the brainstem. Between the brainstem and the cerebrum, is the amygdala. This is a tiny almond-shaped gland that is responsible for storing emotions, packing them away for future reference. Your strongest emotional responses are captured and filed in this deep recess of the brain. We house our most powerful memories here. These are our most significant memories. Because they are linked to heightened emotion, we can recall them both voluntarily, but they also reappear involuntarily.

Storing memory in the amygdala is a handy way to preserve cherished memories of loved ones, but memories can also flood the brain with unpleasant experiences as well. For example, soldiers who witness the atrocities of war experience PTSD when these outrageously negative memories have been re-activated.

The amygdala is also next to the part of the brain responsible for basic survival skills: finding food and water, fight or flight mechanisms, and reproduction. These responses correlate with the two lowest levels on Maslow's hierarchy. The moment the brain feels threatened, all responses revert to the most basic of functions. Everything shifts into first gear. Your hands and brow may become sweaty, your stomach will tie in knots, and you're wondering if you have to fight or flee.

When the brain downshifts into this survival mode, it can't do anything else. The brain will not learn new things, and any self-actualization must be postponed. Self-esteem is the last thing the brain is thinking at this point. It's only worried about survival.

When the brain is certain that any risk or danger has been mitigated, it returns once again to higher cognitive functioning. Less danger, perceived or real, means more opportunity for higher-order thinking, inspiration, and creativity. In fact, the human brain actually craves opportunities for meta-cognition, or thinking about thinking.

The brain also is programmed to value reward. Anytime something positive happens, our gray matter releases oxytocin and dopamine, the two chemicals that reward pleasure. They encourage us to seek out more positives. We feel good when we learn something new or accomplish a task not previously mastered, especially if it's something we know is good for us or for others in our community.

If we help others, we're rewarded with pleasant endorphins. If we lose a few pounds or increase our endurance, we get more endorphins. Those same pleasure-rewarding endorphins are also why we can eat a whole bag of cookies or chips before we realize that we just threw away a week of dieting and exercise. The immediate gratification is too much to pass up.

You may be wondering, what does the brain and all those endorphins have to do with self-esteem?

This brain-based reward system goes hand-in-hand with validation and self-esteem. The more validated we feel, the more oxytocin and dopamine our brains release. Our thoughts create feelings, and feelings cause us to take action. We are encouraged to develop a cycle of thinking, feeling, and doing for continued pleasurable rewards.

Think about the times in your life when you received praise for something you did. Chances are good that you felt so positive about yourself that you sought out more opportunities to show everyone what you were capable of. You kept achieving more because you felt good, and you wanted to preserve that feeling by getting more praise. The praise improved your self-esteem, and you felt confident about yourself.

Then the cycle started all over again.

Validation improves self-esteem and creates the desire for pleasure. The lure of pleasure makes us want to continue the behaviors that released the oxytocin and dopamine in the first place. Our thoughts, feelings, and actions get our needs met, and along the way, we also increase our self-esteem. Knowing how this cycle worked led psychologists to wonder if the process is different between men and women. Does gender affect the inherent amount of self-esteem in males and females? And what about different cultures? If there might be differences in self-esteem levels between men and women, could there also be disparity in self-esteem among diverse cultures?

For both questions, the answer is yes . . . and no.

Gender, Culture and Self-Esteem

We know that thoughts trigger feelings, and those feelings cause us to take action or walk away from a challenge. Much of what we decide either to do or to avoid doing is based on our level of functioning in Maslow's hierarchy.

As we saw, humans take care of their basic needs first. Air, water, and food are our top priorities, followed by the need for shelter and clothing. When these needs are met, we can help others and work on ourselves as well. Our brains reward us for the choices we make by releasing endorphins into our systems. Satisfaction earns us increased levels of dopamine, which in turn, makes us want to continue seeking satisfaction. A satisfying meal nourishes us. We feel fantastic after a good night's sleep. We're pleased when we can help a fellow human being. We're proud of ourselves when we've mastered a new skill.

But are these feelings the same for men and women? Do men and women have similar levels of self-esteem, or is their self-esteem, and thus, their confidence, wildly different?

For quite sometime, people have assumed that gender affects self-esteem levels. After all, men have always been perceived as more confident, stronger, and more able-bodied. There is a tendency to envision men as testosterone-filled creatures who thump their chests in pride. They know what they want from life, and they aim to get it.

Their self-esteem knows no bounds, and they ooze confidence, right? Not really. While some men certainly have tons of confidence, so do some women. Confident women understand why they are successful and what to do if they aren't. They refuse to allow assumptions and limiting beliefs to hold them back. They may not be chest thumpers, but they are certainly just as strong as their male counterparts.

Women display their self-esteem and their confidence in different ways than men.
Even in modern times, a prevailing attitude has suggested that, perhaps, women have lower self-esteem than men. Popular wisdom dictated that men developed far more self-esteem than women. Their confidence completely overshadowed the women's sense of self-reliance.

Researchers conducted numerous studies proving that men had the upper hand when it came to self-esteem, confidence, and courage.

In 2012, Dr. Janet Shibley Hyde, along with Kristen Kling, both from the University of Wisconsin Madison, analyzed hundreds of research studies that had been conducted about the effect of gender on self-esteem. Their research revealed that the gender gap in self-esteem is not as large as it might have once been thought. As it turns out, men and women experience a relatively small disparity when it comes to self-esteem.

The studies revealed that although men had higher self-esteem levels over all, the gap between the levels of the men and women was so small that it was negligible -- insignificant by research standards. There's very little difference in self-esteem between men and women, although men have eked out a negligible lead – about three-tenths of a percentage point.

The real gap is self-esteem lies in age differences. It's adolescents who have some of the widest gaps in self-esteem when compared to others. Teens have lower self-esteem, and they're less confident – regardless of what they insist. Of course, the profound self-esteem gaps begin to close as the teenagers get older. With age comes experience, and that experience produces satisfaction, self-esteem and confidence. Ultimately, middle-aged people and seniors have more self-esteem and show greater confidence than younger people.

Several physiological reasons explain this shift. First of all, teenagers are a kettle of raging hormones as they change from children to adults. Teens experience the growth of body hair, genital development, and extreme mood fluctuations on their way to adulthood, but that's not all. The frontal lobe of their cerebrum Is not yet fully developed. The frontal cortex will not be completely developed for girls until their late teen years; boys won't have a fully developed frontal cortex until their mid-twenties.

No wonder adolescents have less self-esteem than people in other age groups.
Teenagers' bodies are changing rapidly during this time, and they question whether each metamorphosis is normal or not. Uncertainty grips many teens with each transformation they undergo. Even though research studies have confirmed that teens, generally, have less self-esteem than older people, it's important to be cautious in making assumptions about this or any other group. The greatest danger in assuming if self-esteem gaps exist is the assumption itself. By assuming that one group has less self-esteem than another, people may be more likely to create a wider gap by living up to a self-fulfilling prophecy. They instill a limiting belief that can greatly affect self-perception.

Leslie may have grown up thinking she was as capable as the next person, but her dad's limiting beliefs changed all that. His assumptions altered Leslie's sense of self-esteem. She did not develop low self-esteem because she is female. She failed to develop a strong sense of self-esteem during her teenage years – the time when she was most vulnerable – because of her father's limiting beliefs. Leslie learned to believe she had less value than males, even though that wasn't the case. Leslie lived up to her dad's expectations, but the performance bar hadn't been set very high.

Had Professor Hyde been able to measure the gap in self-esteem between Leslie and Leslie's father, the difference likely would have been remarkable, even though Leslie once had as much, if not more, self-esteem than her dad. Her dad made Leslie believe that she was inferior. Leslie lived up to his self-fulfilling prophecy, meeting her father's expectations head-on.
As a result, she experienced low achievement, lacked social skills, and even struggled with depression.

The low self-esteem cycle isn't any more gender-specific than the high-self-esteem cycle is. Men also present with similar symptoms when they experience low self-esteem. Joe is one of these men. Although he hung around the guys, his flagging social skills prevented him from self-advocating just as much as they prevented him from advocating for others.

The disparity in self-esteem is less about gender and more about cultural expectations.

Culture and Self-Esteem

The American Psychological Association in 2016 agreed with Dr. Hyde's research. Adults and older people do have more self-esteem than teenagers. Men experience slightly higher levels of self-esteem, especially after their teenage years. Women, on average, have nearly as much self-esteem as men.

However, one of the most interesting findings was that the self-esteem gap between genders in Western cultures was more pronounced than those of anywhere else. The affluent show the greatest disparity in self-esteem levels. Individualistic behavior can mitigate self-esteem and reduce confidence.

The result is a keeping-up-with-the-Jones effect. Your neighbor has acquired the newest lawnmower or most exclusive designer pup, so you must also rush out to do the same. If you purchase a new car, everyone on your street may feel compelled to update their vehicles. Your self-esteem becomes reliant on your ability to meet community standards defined by material possessions. Self-esteem in these cases is based on meeting unrealistic expectations set by the community.

The smallest gaps of self-esteem and confidence appeared in less affluent communities. People who relied collectively on their community had similar levels of self-esteem and confidence. The collectivist approach to meeting human needs allows for greater self-esteem, regardless of gender. According to the research, European countries and the United States have the most pronounced differences and self-esteem between genders. These communities were among the most affluent when compared to populations in developing countries around the world. Asian countries had the smallest gender differences in self-esteem.

Wendy, for example, lives in one of these more affluent countries driven by personal independence and gain. Her self-esteem was plummeting because of her relentless pursuit of more hours for more money. While she and her husband needed to get back on their feet, at some point, they would meet that goal and then what? Would Wendy continue her pace so they could keep up with the Joneses, whether that competition was real or imagined?

Regardless of the country of origin, though, older people still have greater levels of self-esteem than those who are younger. Age wins every time, but so does collaboration.

Community Validation

Validation, self-esteem and confidence all come back to community.
Those with whom we surround ourselves have the biggest impact on our lives.

Psychologists once assumed self-esteem was based on personal value. That's not quite true. Society's expectations and our ability to meet our culture's standards have the greatest influence on self-esteem and thus, our confidence.

Self-esteem is actually more extrinsically based than it is intrinsic. Our external world influences our behavior. Norms and customs shape our behavior. Those people who can change themselves to meet these expectations are more likely to have greater levels of self-esteem. On the other hand, our inability to meet these standards reduces our likelihood for self-esteem, regardless of gender or even age. We want to know that we are living up to the expectations set before us. What changes is our perception that we are on track.

If a culture values independence, its members base self-esteem on the ability to achieve independence. Likewise, if you grow up in a culture that values respecting elders, you will base your self-esteem on your ability to demonstrate that respect. The same process works in micro-communities as well. While there is a larger community standard, there are also smaller microcosms that dictate standards for behavior. For Leslie, it was her parents' family values, especially her dad's.

In Joe's case, his micro-community was his group of friends. They set a standard of braggadocio and bullying that Joe felt uncomfortable joining in. Joe developed low self-esteem because he could not – or would not—meet his friend's standards of behavior.

And finally, Wendy isolated herself with her work until she felt as though she could never meet the standards she that she imagined existed. She saw only long hours ahead, and she ticked them off one by one. She would continue until she finished her job or collapsed in the pursuit of elusive validation. This validation could be achieved only by accomplishing her community's standards.

What we perceive as valuable and worthy of validation affects our ability to produce self-esteem. It's possible to validate your own actions, but we seek affirmation from others within our community. We want to know that we are part of a group because it is the group that helps us meet our needs. They validate our actions, and when that happens, the chemicals in our brains affirm that we're on our way to building self-esteem and increasing our confidence.

Not best, but different

No one culture is less or more *"right"* in what it values. Each culture is unique, and there is no right or wrong in their approach to validation and self-esteem. Some people may disagree, but there is no better age to be. Each age is unique and full of benefits as well as shortcomings. You are no more predisposed to self-esteem and confidence if you are a man than if you are a woman.

Your self-esteem and confidence comes from understanding the role your community plays in your life. They are dependent on how you train your brain to think, what you allow yourself to feel, and what actions you take. You are responsible for generating the circumstances for your validation. Our next chapter will show how you can use physical, intellectual, emotional and spiritual dimensions to increase your self-esteem and formulate confidence.

The 4 Dimensions and Your Role in Each One

Begin with the Blueprint

If you've ever built a home or even assembled a product, you know how important it is to figure out what the biggest pieces are, and deal with them first. It seems like once you know where to begin, all the other slotted pieces fall into place.

That's true for assembling a child's swing set, building a tool shed, or constructing a new home. With every project, you begin with the most important pieces first, and everything else almost takes care of itself. All you have to do is follow the blueprint, or directions, when you get started.

A rule of thumb like this is especially true when building up your self-esteem and forging confidence. For that reason, this book offers you a set of directions. It's a blueprint, if you will, for assembling and maintaining your self-esteem and growing confidence.

Just as with any building, the work begins with the cornerstone. In our case, there are four of them. The cornerstones of your self-esteem consist of four dimensions: the Physical, the Intellectual/Mental, the Emotional, and the Spiritual. Think of these four dimensions as the cornerstones that make up your house. They are indispensable to your make up.

A cornerstone is the first piece installed when erecting a building. It's the lynchpin against which all other stones are laid, regardless of how big or tall your building will be. Cornerstones have their own uniqueness, and they are the link to all of the other components. Although each one can stand alone, it is stronger when used in conjunction with the three others. Together, they create an impenetrable fortress called your self-esteem. When your self-esteem is strong, your confidence is unshakeable.

The kind of character that inspires confidence is built much the same way you would construct your house. You can't toss around boundaries and tilt up your walls without determining the cornerstones of your character. You must know what you stand for, what boundaries you intend to set and keep, and continuously measure your self-esteem. This is how you build the courage of your convictions. Most people are pretty good about establishing strong foundations in one or two of the dimensions, but they may let the others go, focusing instead on what matters most to them. Traditionally, the most important things get our attention and require our effort.

It's critical to work on all four dimensions. Each of these cornerstones is like the leg of a stool. One- and two-legged stools are quasi-functional, but three-legged stools is far sturdier. The four-legged stool is the sturdiest of all.

Imagine how strong – and confident – you would feel if you strengthened your position in each dimension, or cornerstone. Imagine how you would feel if you could stand on the four-legged stool instead of having to balance precariously on the one-legged stool.

Defining yourself in all four dimensions and maintaining your sense of self takes time and thoughtfulness, but you can do it. You can identify and create strong cornerstones that will allow you to build your self-esteem, strengthen and be confident in the actions you take.

Let's look at each dimension individually.

The Physical Dimension

Ernestine Shepherd knows a thing or two about fitness. She devotes her days to getting exercise, including a brisk 10-mile walk and weight training. She eats fruit, vegetables, and lean protein, quaffing raw egg whites and plenty of water in between meals. Ernie, as she likes to be called, embarked on her fitness journey at a more youthful age of 56, thanks to the encouragement of her younger sister, Velvet. Like most of us, the sisters were getting older, and they just wanted to get in shape.

Although she almost gave up several times, Ernie became the world's oldest female competitive bodybuilder in 2011 at the age of 80, and she's still going strong. She eats nutritious foods, gets the rest she needs, and inspires others to reach their potential physically. She's not alone in her pursuit of fitness and good health. E. Wilma Conner recently earned the title of *"oldest female bodybuilder;"* she's one year older than Ernestine.

So, what's the deal? Do you have to be a bodybuilder or a senior (or both?) to be in great shape? Hardly.

You don't have to be any of those to be strong and in good physical health. Establishing a strong presence in the physical dimension comes from giving your body the healthy things it needs. Ernie and Wilma figured out what that took for their bodies, and they did it. You can, too.

Let's start at the beginning with an inventory of your overall physical fitness.

Although physical fitness means something different for everyone, generally speaking, those who are fit physically can answer in the affirmative to these four questions:

Do you have enough energy to do your job and leisure activities you love?
Do you get enough sleep at night to feel rested during the day?
Do you eat nutritious foods?
Can you ward off most colds and illnesses on your own?

If you said yes each, time, congratulations! You've got a foundation of physical health established. You're active, rested, nourished, and healthy.

But if you said, *"occasionally,"* *"sometimes,"* or *"nope,"* to any of the questions, it may be time to focus on developing healthy practices when it comes to your physical well-being. Let's explore how you can do that.

The Physical Dimension of Good Living

Good health is your physical foundation, and it's so vital that it impacts all of the other cornerstones of your life.

People with good health find that they are better at handling stress and warding off illness. If you can maintain a weight suitable for your height and frame, you'll be less likely to suffer from chronic heart disease, high blood pressure, and even creaky knees that want to give out every time you stand up.

That same good health will give you more satisfaction when it comes to participating in the activities you love. You'll find it easier to tackle simple physical tasks, whether that means puttering in the garden, emptying the trash, or squatting to pick something up.

Being physically healthy isn't an elusive unicorn, to be captured by only a lucky few. Good health is for everyone, and it can be yours. You've heard the drill before. Watch your diet, get plenty of exercise, and lay off the things that are bad for you. That advice sounds almost too simple to put into practice. But it works!

The challenge is in keeping the momentum going. Losing the first ten pounds makes it more tempting to reward yourself with pizza or chips. Did you jog 10 kilometers this week or hit the gym six days in a row? You deserve a break, so you reward yourself with the very thing you're trying to avoid. You may have skipped seconds on the ice cream when everyone else was gorging, or gave up the cigs, but how are you sabotaging your efforts to become more healthy?

If you sabotage yourself enough, good, healthy habits will never form. The American writer Mark Twain once remarked that it's easy to quit smoking. He himself had done it thousands of times. Good health habits are the result of perseverance.

The problem is that perseverance won't take root until you've committed the same action 30 times in a row. When what you do becomes a habit, you're on you're way to a healthy lifestyle.

So where do you start? At the beginning, with simple steps. Let's get to work!

Diet: you are what you eat

The first area to address is diet, but we're not discussing which weight loss program you're on. There are hundreds of weight loss programs and gimmicks; they aren't our focus. We're talking about what you eat, in general.

Listen to the two statements below. Which one best describes your day?

Statement 1: Breakfast? What breakfast? The day began in a rush, but I have to grab my morning coffee before I get to the office. There can be no day ahead without caffeine; occasionally I add a biscuit or breakfast sandwich to my order. Lunch is usually fast food, perhaps even the quickest meal of all, a candy bar or package of vending machine crackers. They're small packages; so sometimes in the late afternoon, I need a second snack. When I get home, I'm starving; I eat whatever I want, including seconds.

Statement 2: I eat a big breakfast, and it's the full meal deal: eggs, bacon or sausage, potatoes, toast, and sometimes a pancake or two. It's the most important meal of the day, after all. I skip lunch, so I try to eat dinner by 7:00 p.m., but often, it's later when I eat. I'm pretty good about most meals, but I do love pasta and cream sauce, with plenty of garlic bread. After that, I fall asleep on the couch before bedtime.

Do you identify with Statement 1 or Statement 2?
If you are most like Statement 1, you find yourself rushed throughout the day, and your nutrition takes a back seat to everything else. Actually, what you're eating may not be giving you the nutrition you need to fuel your work throughout the day. You begin with caffeine and sometimes fat and sugar. By midday, you add more fat and sugar into your system, and you find yourself in an energy slump in the afternoon. When you finally take time for yourself,

you're eating anything just to have something, but none of it has been nutritious.

People who identify with Statement 2 have the right intentions by starting the day with protein, but they feast in the morning and fast throughout the rest of the day, ignoring their needs, and then splurge on rich and creamy starches. They fall fast asleep in a carb-induced coma.

So what should you be doing?

Try eating many small, healthy portions throughout the day. Five or six small meals can be beneficial to your health because they'll keep you fueled -- and away from the vending machines. We're not going to ask you to count calories or carb grams (yet), but we do suggest mini-meals like these:

Breakfast: Fruit that comes in it own wrapper (apples, bananas, oranges, etc.), an egg-white omelet, oatmeal or other wholesome grain, a sourdough muffin or toast with peanut butter.

Lunch: A salad or vegetables, lean protein, and a small portion of carbs, such as a potato (baked, not fried).

Snacks: Cheese sticks, small portions of nuts, veggie sticks, or fruit.

Dinner: A salad or vegetables, lean protein, and a small portion of carbs, such as brown rice.

A good diet is about variety, balance and portion control. Rather than starve yourself by counting calories, eat less of what's fattening or sugary and more of what's healthy, like vegetables.

The trick lies not only in eating what you like, but being prepared to eat healthily regardless of the situation you find yourself in. You don't have to slurp egg white concoctions between meals like Ernie if you can't stand the thought of drinking raw eggs, but you should at least commit to something nutritious.

But there's no time for that, you cry. You *have* to make the time, and you can. You *are* worth the effort!

Did a late meeting cause you to miss lunch? If you have a bag of nuts or container of fruit on hand, that may be enough to get to your next meal. Busy week ahead? Prep your meals and snacks ahead of time so you can grab and go – or heat up your dinner when you get home. Having something prepared ahead of time reduces the likelihood that you'll eat something a lot less healthy.

Just be sure to use a smaller plate! It's crazy, but plates sizes have expanded to match our expanding waistlines. In the last century, plates measured a generous seven to nine inches across. Today, plates can be as big as thirteen inches in diameter! Huge plates make us miscalculate the amount of food we need. Switch to a smaller plate size, and you could find yourself switching to a small pant size as well. Do you have to give up everything you love? Of course not.

We have a colleague who refuses to give up chocolate for any reason. If you offer her anything with chocolate, she will accept it – and eat it. The caveat is that she eats only one piece of candy or one bite, and she does her best to practice good living habits with (almost) everything else.

So do this right now: think about one thing you can change in your diet. Commit to that one change in your diet. Prep your own snack bags. Get out the smaller plates. Switch to water, and drink one less carbonated beverage every day.

Pick that one thing and do it for the next 30 days.

Exercise: body in motion stays in motion

Now that you're more conscientious about the fuel you're putting into your body, it's time to get moving. Let's exercise.

If you are already physically active, good for you! Your next step in keeping fit might be to join a club or hire a personal trainer. You may even want to skip this section, because we're going to talk about taking the first steps in getting moving and staying motivated.

If your exercise plan has consisted of one sit up a day – getting up in the morning and lying down at night – it's time to add rigor to your workout. Actually, it's time to develop a workout plan.
Exercise requires movement, intensity and duration.

Sitting on the couch and thumbing the remote control buttons may require duration, but not much movement or intensity. A couple of jumping jacks or cartwheels will get you moving, and they'll have the intensity you need, but they lack duration.

Again, it's about developing good habits over time. The best exercise plan is the one you can sustain.

A wise yoga teacher once had a studio where she offered what she called *"the yoga you need."* She told newcomers that she wanted them to try the yoga positions to the best of their ability. There was no pressure to perfect the awkward standing-at-a-tilt-on-one-leg-wispy-phoenix-rising-from-a-yoga-mat pose. The teacher recognized that everyone had their own needs for movement, intensity, and duration. Every student honed their skills – developing the habit of regular exercise over time, according to need.

Yoga may not be your thing. That's okay. There are plenty of other activities for you to try, such as bicycling, kayaking, skiing, swimming, skating, golfing, weight-lifting, and playing ball. But perhaps you're not ready for these more aggressive physical pursuits.

If you don't have the stamina (or funds) for these, there's still walking, which is one of the best exercises you can do. Best of all, it's free.

A good goal for beginners is to work up to about 10,000 steps per day. That's the equivalent of about three miles. Ace this number and you can increase your goals. Every trip to the laundry room, the break room, and across the Little League field counts. So does going up and down the stairs and walking in from further distances in the parking lot.

You could guesstimate the distance you're walking, but there's an easier, more accurate way to count your daily steps. Steppers can choose from a variety of step-counting devices. Digital counters send your stats to your computer so you can analyze your progress over time. You can also use a stand-alone device. For a less than the cost of a lunch, you can purchase a step counter that will tally your progress and keep you motivated.

What's important is that you get moving. If logging 10,000 steps seems impossible, aim for something less daunting.

When you can consistently hit the mark for ten days in a row, increase your goal.

Today, take your first steps toward fitness. Keep stepping in the right direction for the next thirty days. And remember that a body set in motion ***stays*** in motion.

The Quality of Life you Deserve

Getting a handle on your lifestyle may be a little more challenging because changing ingrained habits is something easier said than done. It's a fine thing to imagine having the best of intentions, only to fall off the wagon time after time – like Mark Twain. You already know the standard advice about changing your lifestyle: stop smoking, drink less, get rid of the recreational drugs. The question is *how* do you do it?

Let's use smoking as an example. It's a habit that affects not only you, but those around you, in the form of second-hand smoke. It's not only life-threatening, but costly, so many smokers try to give up cigarettes. Nearly two-thirds of smokers who try to quit attempt going cold turkey. They try never to pick up another cigarette. Slightly more than twenty percent of them succeed.

Some people find that substituting one activity for another helps. For example, if you're trying to cut back on smoking, substitute gum for cigarettes or consider vaping instead. Other people seek medical intervention, and many have found support groups, both online and in their communities, helpful. You can use similar strategies for any other addiction, including overeating.

No one intervention works every time for everyone. In fact, many people find that a combination of strategies helps them beat unhealthy lifestyle habits. The change begins with you. For any strategy to work, you must want to make the change.

Sleep: let's get some shut-eye

An area many people ignore when it comes to improving their lifestyle is sleep. On average, adults need seven to nine hours of pillow time – solid, uninterrupted sleep. No lying in bed watching the television, reading email, or playing games on your tablet while waiting to fall asleep.

Yes, there are individuals like Ernie Sheldon who function well on just a few hours of sleep a night, especially as they age, but most people are more like Wendy, from our first chapter. They need far more sleep than they are getting.

No wonder. The twenty-four hours we have each day seems like very little time to do everything we need and want to get done, so we carve out extra time by chipping away at our sleep time. We borrow minutes and hours from the time needed for rejuvenation, and most of us never pay back the account in full.

You may be able to function on very little sleep, but lack of sleep can impair your ability to think, perform complex tasks, and interpret communication. It wears down your body. You see, while you're asleep, your brain is at work. It works with your body to release the hormones you need, repair any damage to your tissues or muscles, improve your memory, and even regulate your appetite. Getting enough sleep can help you reduce your cravings!

Finding your sleep set point is easy. When you go to bed tonight, don't set your alarm. Note the time you turn in and when you wake up. That's how much sleep you need. Your body will wake you up naturally when it's ready. If you can't afford to sleep in tomorrow morning, perform the test on a day that you can sleep later without consequence.

Once you know how much sleep you need, plan your next day backward. Determine the time you must get up in order to start your day. Subtract the hours your body needs for sleep, and that's your bedtime. To make the commitment to a full night's sleep, set a bedtime alarm as a reminder that it's time for shut-eye.

Diet, exercise, healthy lifestyle habits, and sleep.

If you commit to taking one step toward improving each area, you'll feel better and look better. You don't have to make big changes. You don't even have to make them all at once. You just have to decide on your new habit and keep it up for thirty days.

Hopefully, you've already been thinking, *"I can do that!"* You can!

This advice is meant to give you a good running start toward becoming healthier. Don't use it to replace what your physician told you to do. Use our tips as a springboard to building a strong cornerstone of physical health.

A good physical foundation will improve your self-esteem and help you develop the confidence to become courageous.

In the chapters ahead, we'll check in on how you're doing with your new habits, and we'll dig deeper into specifics as well. In the meantime, attend to your new habits daily.

The Intellectual/Mental Dimension

You've embarked on improving the most critical cornerstone of your foundation, the physical dimension, so now it's time to turn to the next one: your intellectual/mental dimension.

Intellect is more than an IQ or how much school you've had. Intellect combines thinking, understanding, reasoning and evaluating – skills you need to be successful, confident and courageous. Some of these skills are taught, and some you acquire through experience. Anyone can master these skills and keep them sharp at any age. Mental acuity comes from curiosity. It's when we have an insatiable hunger to know to more about the world around us that we feed our brain with information. Your brain loves to learn.

The brain is constantly changing itself and adapting according to the information it receives. The more information, the more neural pathways your brain will create. It's trying to create a dense infrastructure of useful information rather than rely on a single pathway. The denser network is faster and more resilient, which is important when you're working on your self-esteem. The more you learn, the more connections your brain cells make between themselves. When your learning stagnates, you have fewer connections. Those that do exist become isolated.

Your job is to feed your brain, much the way you feed your body: with nourishment.

Your brain wants more than an arsenal of facts. Anyone can memorize encyclopedic entries. It's how you make connections with information that improves intellect. To develop your intellectual dimension, you'll have to use some higher order thinking skills like analysis, evaluation, and synthesis.

Many people find working simple math and language puzzles to be an enjoyable experience. Both Sodoku and crossword puzzles serve to engage the brain in new ways. After all, how many people can identify a three-letter word for a bird that can't fly? Once figure out that the puzzle is talking about an emu, you're going to want to see a picture of that, and you may even pause to consider how far removed it is from an ostrich. That's curiosity at work.

Other people find that their hobbies keep them mentally alert. Wood-carving, painting, playing an instrument, sewing, working on mechanical engines, playing chess – they all keep the brain active and engaged. So does traveling, reading, taking online classes, and writing. The list of things to do is virtually endless; you just have to pick something that interests you, and do it. Regardless of the hobby you pick or the topic you want to know more about, there are four steps to take if you're serious about improving your intellect. These steps include starting with yourself, looking at both sides, predicting the next steps, and asking why and what if.

Imagine that your local school system wants to build a new school. Residents in the community have become heated up about the prospect, and they have been polarizing into two camps for the last few weeks. One group is highly committed to the project, and they insist the new campus is necessary. The other group is against adding another school building.

Let's use the four steps to think through the issue.

First, start with yourself. What's your initial take on the situation? Are you for or against the new school? What reasons can you give to justify your response?

Next, look at both sides. How will those who are in favor of the new school going to benefit? Will anyone else benefit as well? And what about those who are opposed? Are their reasons justified? For example, if the school is built, how will the cost impact the community? Do the benefits outweigh the cost or the imminent changes in traffic patterns near the school? Would the children be better served with a new building?

Third, predict what you think will happen next. Which side has the more compelling argument? Is it possible that anyone could stop them and alter the outcome? Then what would happen?

Finally, ask why and what if. Why is the school necessary in the first place? What would happen if it was built? What would happen if it wasn't built?

You can apply this same thinking process to anything, from issues in the news to how to improve the skills you need for your hobby. Improving your intellectual and mental dimension is about learning how to problem-solve. It requires analysis, evaluation, and synthesis to be effective. Strengthen your mental acuity through meta-cognition. That means tame the time to think about how you're thinking.

To get started, try keeping a meta-cognition journal. On the left side of the page, describe the issue you're thinking about. Worry less about grammar and spelling and more about capturing the information. You don't even have to write in sentences. List items, make bullet points, draw pictures to help explain. Work through each of the four steps of critical thinking (starting with yourself, looking at both sides, predicting the next steps, and asking why and what if).

On the right side page of the journal, reflect on the process you used to come up with your evaluation. What surprised you, either about what you uncovered in your pursuit of facts about the issue, or how you responded, and if you possibly changed your mind? Let your responses on this page be like stream-of-consciousness writing, where you write down whatever you're thinking about.

By interacting in writing several times a week, you'll begin to formulate a habit of thinking through the four steps. As this habit becomes ingrained, you'll find yourself thinking through each of the steps without having to write anything down. You will have cemented and strengthened your intellectual/mental dimension.

The Emotional Dimension

You have forty-two unique muscles in your face. Use these muscles in combination with each other or in isolation, and you can produce a considerable amount of complex emotional responses, just with your face. So how many emotions could you reveal with your facial muscles?

Some researchers will tell you there are twenty-seven different categories of emotions, and other researchers have decided there are only four basic emotions, period. What most people do agree on is that emotions are negative or positive reactions to the thoughts we've been thinking. It's true. Your thoughts determine your emotions, and your emotions determine your actions. That means that your feelings really do play a critical part is how you show up every day, and it's why emotions make up the third cornerstone of your well-being and self-esteem.

Some of the most basic emotions take the form of fear, anger, sadness, happiness, acceptance, surprise, and joy. You can take an inventory of how and when these emotions appear in your life by writing your answers to the questions after each description.

The first three emotions are negative. They aren't necessarily bad, but if not used to your advantage, they can destroy your self-esteem.

Fear is the feeling you get when your brain tells to prepare to flee or fight. Your senses heighten so you can analyze threats to your safety, and your body prepares itself to react accordingly. Make a list of what you fear the most. How could you lessen those fears?

Anger can be just as strong as fear, but it comes from displeasure when something has not gone how you thought it would. When allowed to boil over, anger can be dangerous to yourself and to others. What makes you angry?

Sadness comes from real or perceived loss. Yearning for something that no longer exists or is no longer possible can leave you with an empty feeling. What has caused you the greatest sadness?

The next two emotions are more positive.

Happiness occurs at times of pleasure. You derive pleasure from what meets your needs. List the times you are most happy. What about them made you happy? How can you have more of these experiences?

Acceptance takes place when you are content enough with yourself to let go of judgment and evaluation. That's pretty hard to do. Name a time when you avoided judging another and accepted them for who they were. What were the circumstances and the results?

The last two emotions can be the most difficult to achieve, but they are the most satisfying.

Surprise, also known as delight, enchants us. It catches us off guard and reminds us of the whimsy and miracles that exist in the world. When was the last time you were surprised? What happened, and how did it make you feel? What did you do afterward?

Joy is the most elusive emotion, but it's the one athletes and artists know intimately. That's because they find joy when doing what it is that they love best: competing or creating. It's what's known as *"being in the zone."* They lose all track of time, and they are less aware of their surroundings. They have a singular, laser-like focus on what they are doing. What do you do that makes you experience joy? How often do you allow joyfulness? What's stopping you from having more joy?

Most people don't experience only one or two emotions in a day. They may find themselves angry about morning rush hour traffic, surprised to have an *"at-a-boy"* from the boss, accepting that the box lunch won't taste any better than the container it came in, and happy that they meet their daily/weekly/monthly goals. And these are only a handful of the emotions you could experience in a single morning. Your emotions rise and fall in response to what you are thinking.

Emotions also dictate how you will react to a situation. Being negative *(fearful, angry, or sad)* will consume more of your energy than any of the other emotions if you let it. These three emotions will weigh you down and prevent you from choosing better courses of action.

Does that mean you should never be afraid or angry about something? Of course not. In our opinion, the person who discovers a gnarly-looking tarantula hiding in their sock drawer is justified in jumping back in fear. What's important is how you use your fear of that spider to determine your next action.

You could close the drawer and never wear socks again. Or you could use your fear to make sure you never have a face-to-face meeting like that again. You'd call a pest exterminator, or you'd clean out the chest of drawers to make sure there were no other crawly surprises lurking among your garments. Your emotions are yours alone. They don't belong to anyone else. Your ability to control them will determine your level of confidence. If you want to be courageous, you must know how to use your emotions to solidify your self-esteem and give you the confidence you need.

<u>Here's how to get your emotions to work for you</u>

Overturn fear by seeking wisdom. We fear the things we least understand. That's' why it's critical to shore up your intellectual/mental dimension. Remember the tarantula? If you knew that tarantulas are pretty harmless to humans, you may react a little differently to the creepy arachnid.

The fact that you are unlikely to die from a tarantula bite may help you harness your response and use it to improve your circumstances: namely, to get rid of the spider.

Use anger to define and set healthy boundaries. Anger happens when a boundary has been crossed – either you crossed someone else's boundary or they crossed yours. Look at your anger and determine if it is helping you take positive action, or if it is holding you back. If it's holding you back, you'll need to explore why the issue is so important. What's preventing you from letting go? Remember that you have the right to be mad, but not to be violent. If you feel like hurting yourself or someone else, seek help immediately.

Let sadness help you create memories. Everyone of us will experience sadness, but we don't have to live there. Sadness has a place in our lives. Accept sadness for what it is, and thank it for creating the memories you have. Then turn to other pursuits.

Use happiness to guide your actions. When you are happy, the positive vibes affect others. In fact, happiness is the emotion that's most contagious. You can pass it along to other people. Identify the times when you are happy. What kind of thoughts go through your head? What is your body doing? If you re-enact these conditions, you are more likely to experience happiness more often. You condition yourself to respond with happiness.

Practice acceptance by not judging others. It's easy to judge other by our own standards, but our job isn't to judge. We don't have to evaluate what someone else does or doesn't do. We tend to evaluate others by our own standards. That' not fair or equitable for the other person. He or she cannot be you; only you can be you. You can dislike someone else's actions without judging them, but don't expect them to live their lives according to your standards. You will both fall short, and so will your self-esteem.

Look for surprise in the small things. A flower that blooms in an unexpected place, a small kindness, the first snowflake of the season – look for and savor whatever that tiny blessing might be. Avoid being so busy that you cannot connect with another person, offering a helping hand, a greeting, or even a smile.

Experience joy when doing what you love. Give yourself permission to focus on what you're doing, to the exclusion of everything else. Do what it is that you love to do, and do it often. Be in the moment and in the zone for as long as you can.

If you permit other people to tell you which emotions you should feel, you're in danger of eroding your self-esteem. They cannot experience what you are experiencing because they are not you. They do not dictate or control your emotions. Only you can do that.

Know that every one of your emotions and feelings are normal. It is natural to feel fear, anger, sadness, happiness, acceptance, surprise and joy, as well as many more feelings. It's okay to be emotional.

We each experience a wide range of emotions throughout the day, and there's nothing wrong with experiencing any of them. Our emotions simply are, like the color of our eyes or the shape of our hands. What matters is what you do with the emotions you have. We can use our emotions to dig in our feet and refuse to grow as a person, or we can continue to develop our emotional cornerstone to build self-esteem and confidence.

Recognizing your emotions can help you complete the though-feeling-action sequence. In the end, you'll be stronger and more confident for it.

Not What You Might Expect

This is not a book on religion, but spirituality has its place both in this chapter and among the cornerstones that make you who you are. The fourth and final dimension is your spirituality.

For some people, that may mean a belief in a higher power, God, a Supreme Being who controls the universe and all things in it. This belief can be practiced through adherence to a religion, or it may be practiced through self-reflection.

Either way, the practitioner reflects on the soul, or the metaphysical aspect of our selves. It's about being part of something bigger than a blip on a timeline, and most humans ponder not only their existence but also their impact on the planet and the lives of those around them.

Regardless of the way in which you practice spirituality, it's important that you be spiritual. Spirituality guides your code of ethics. If you think it's wrong to steal, you won't do it. It's not that you are incapable of theft, but you are unwilling to compromise your morals. Doing so is not part of your spiritual nature.

Being spiritual means focusing on things that are intangible. You focus less on material objects and focus more on a higher plane of thinking – the metaphysical plane, where the soul exists. So how do you build this dimension so that it is as strong as the other three?

You can strengthen your spirituality with these tips:

Commit to daily prayer and meditation. Prayer and meditation encourage your brain to slow down and focus on one thing at a time. This exercise can be a welcome relief when you have a busy schedule because it allows you to slow down. During these few minutes, pray by giving thanks and asking for what you need, repeat a single word or phrase over and over, or listen to a relaxation script. Allow your breathing to slow down and become both regular and deep. Avoid multi-tasking during this time.

Listen to your intuition. Logic is a fierce, A-type personality determined to have its way. The black-and-white rules of logic appeal to those who want to know the one right answer. Unfortunately, life isn't like that. There often is no one right answer. It's messy, colorful, and full of creativity and emotion. That's why you should also listen to your intuition. It's okay to do what your brain tells you to do, but take time to listen to what's in your heart. That where playfulness and inspiration live.

Practice forgiveness. Holding a grudge against another person hurts us more than it does the other person. It's been said that having a grudge is like drinking poison and expecting the other guy to get sick. To get rid of a grudge, write your grievance on a piece of paper. Says everything you'd like to say, grit, dirt and all, no matter how ugly – get it out once and for all. Then strike a match to the paper and let your grievance go up in flames. By letting go, you're letting yourself move on. Turn the other cheek. Forgive. And then move forward.

Engage all of your senses. Our fast-paced lives prevent us from enjoying what we do. We wolf down meals, dash to meetings, and get our chores done even though we're so exhausted we're not thinking about what we're doing. Make the mundane memorable by using all five of your sense to enjoy the task at hand. Notice the texture of your food, the sounds you hear on the way to your meeting, and the smell of the laundry detergent.

Purge and start fresh. Getting rid of the clutter you've accumulated means freeing up your space for simple living. If you haven't used a piece of clothing in the last twelve months, donate it or toss it. The same goes with the bric-a-brac you collect: dried up pens, chipped figurines, damaged sporting equipment. You'll have less cleaning to do, and you'll have more time for doing what you love. Treat your body the same by soaking in a tub, exfoliating, and cleansing your hair and skin.

Recite scripture, a quote, or a mantra. Words can be comforting, especially if they are holy or have special significance. They are a welcome reminder of the greater good that exists in the world, and they can raise our self-esteem and bolster our courage. Find the scripture or quote that appeals most to you. Learn it and then recite it daily.

Experience nature. If you're in an office all day, how much do you get to enjoy the outdoors? At the next opportunity to walk in the park, go camping, or trek to the shore, practice using all five of your senses. Stop long enough to identify what you see, hear, smell, taste and touch.

Stop what you're doing. Breathe in deeply. Hold it, two, three, four. And exhale. Repeat nine more times. Feel better?

Be grateful. Believe it or not, being grateful can improve all of your other dimensions: physical, intellectual, and emotional. Being grateful shows you the reason for going on with your life and wanting to be a part of others' lives. To find the blessings in your life, write down one thing for which you are grateful. Do this daily.

Strengthening your spirituality does more for you than boost your self-esteem. It helps you develop the kind of compassion that increase the self-esteem of others. That kind of self-esteem builds confidence!

In Summary

If you devote thirty days to changing your physical habits, and you actively engage with your intellectual, emotional and spiritual self, you will discover that you are strengthening the cornerstones that make you who you are. You are shoring up your self-esteem and fortifying your house. Once it's in place, it will be the fortress where your confidence and courage live.

Developing the cornerstones of your self-esteem requires dedication and perseverance. It takes time, and you'll need to put in the effort. Some days will be harder than others, but the benefits you'll reap are worth the struggle. Keep up your courage, even when all you want to do is follow the path of least resistance.

After ten, twenty, and thirty days, go back and read what you've written in your journal. Notice how the content has changed each time. You're growing as a person, and so is your self-esteem.

Convenience vs. Courage

As you develop new, healthier habits for the for dimensions of your being (cornerstone, house) you may find yourself tempted to choose the path of least resistance. It's an easy road, for sure, and we've all been there are some point in our lives.

We've been too tired to exercise, or we forgot to have something healthy to eat on hand. Exhaustion and hunger made the easier way out more appealing. We took it, and we were grateful. Easy means no effort. No conflict, no anxiety, no stress.

Leaning toward convenience won't kill you, but it won't make your life better, either. It may even have a negative impact. Sound like a surprising concept? For most people, it is.

Convenience over courage shows up in other places as well. Conventional wisdom suggests that it's best to take the path of least resistance. A lack of action is convenient. You don't have to exert any energy. There's no commitment. The easiest choice is often the one presents the least amount of difficulty. We're programmed to make decisions based on two things: safety and convenience.

No wonder. You've already learned that your physical needs are a top priority. Securing shelter, water and food are critical for your existence. You won't survive without them. But for survival to be attainable, you must also have convenience. You cannot spend all for preparing to be a better hunter/fighter. You must also have downtime, time for improving your game.

We've been taught all of our lives to go with the flow. Accept the status quo, and when in Rome, do as the Romans do. The last thing you want to do, we're told, is to make waves. Those swells will rock not only your boat but everyone else's.

It's true that a ship is safe in the harbor, but that's not what a ship is meant for. You are not intended for a life without strife, either. The problem with safety and convenience is that while you'll be safe and your life will be one of convenience, will you truly live? What value will your life have if, like the ship, you stay in port? You're going to have to leave the safety of the harbor and travel out in the world.

This story illustrates this point.
One afternoon, a man noticed a burgeoning cocoon. Inside the small container, an Emperor Moth had completed its transformation and was ready to emerge from the tight quarters binging its body and wings. The insect struggled from within the close confines, trying to gain purchase and get out through a small opening in the shell. The man took pity on the creature. He carefully pulled back the layers of the chrysalis, releasing the exquisite moth.

"There you go, my friend, the world is yours to discover," he said.

The moth lay in a heap, unable to move.

"Go! Shoo! You are free to do whatever you want!" said the man.

Still, the moth did not move. It could not even spread its wings to take flight.

By enabling the moth to take the path of least resistance, the man limited the moth's future. It would never be able to catch the wind with its wings and take to the air. The unhealthy insect would die within the next few hours.

Forcing its own way out of the shell would have made the difference. By pushing through the cocoon's casing, the moth would have pushed the fluid from its body into the wing structure, filling the veins so they could stretch outward and pull the wings taut. The struggle was necessary not only for the moth's growth, but for its very survival.

You cannot spread your wings and take flight with confidence unless you also experience struggle. Resistance grows both muscle and character. The question is, how do you create the experiences you need without endangering your life?

Generating action-oriented courage means being open to new experiences and learning how to derive satisfaction along the way. To do that, you'll need open-mindedness mixed with a healthy dose of both happiness and dissatisfaction.

Unless you are dissatisfied with your progress, you will not seek the kinds of new experiences that bring you satisfaction.

How To Gain Experience and Lose Your Fear

Fear takes root in the unknown

Not knowing how something works can be scary stuff. That's why doctors encourage moms-to-be to learn as much as possible about childbirth. Knowing what to expect during each trimester is helpful to new mothers, but knowing about the stages of birth can alleviate not only fear but also some of the pain associated with the experience. The more they know, the less fear and pain they experience.

If you're ready to embrace new experiences, commit to these three rules for living a rich life:

The more you know, the more you'll grow

Learn as much as you can about your situation. Afraid of flying? Try taking a flying lesson. The hour you spend with a certified pilot, either in the air or in a simulator, can help you better understand how planes work. The appreciation you develop may make your next flight more enjoyable.

Learning at any age keeps your mind alert and agile. Your new experiences may come from taking dance or painting classes, joining a club, or volunteering your time to a worthy cause. Focus less on whether you have the talent for the endeavor and more about what you can discover about the experience and yourself.

Ask yourself:

- What's one benefit I could get from this experience?
- How might it benefit others?
- What new information or skill can I put to use?

Run in the opposite direction

Entrepreneurs demonstrate a real knack for avoiding herd mentality. They understand that if someone is telling you about the next *"get rich scheme,"* it's too late. The only one getting rich is the salesman who is capitalizing on what large groups of people want. Experience and the satisfaction derived from it come from your willingness to take a risk. Do the opposite of what others expect.

You may run into people who tell you, *"impossible," "crazy,"* or worse, but those who went in a different direction had the biggest impact on the world. Some risked a lot to pursue their dreams, and others took on smaller risks. Without risk of any kind, however, your wings won't stretch, and you won't find fulfillment.

Some people like to do what's popular, and they follow the trends set by others. A majority mindset won't give you a meaningful life. It will provide you with mediocrity. Only you can count the measure of your music, especially if you choose to follow the beat of a different drummer.
Ask yourself:

- What is the average mindset about this problem?
- How can I solve it differently?
- What knowledge, time, resources, and skills do I have to make it happen?
- Who else should be involved?

Unproven is unfulfilled

Thinking you're capable and knowing you're capable are two different matters

Confidence comes from the assurance that you can do whatever you set your mind to. Only one out of four people dare to travel independently. They are willing to embark on new experiences, savoring both the good and the bad. The solo travelers don't want to miss a thing. The other three out of four people want to travel with friends or family; they prefer going in a group or not going at all. If that means they miss out, then so be it.

Proving you can travel on your own is perhaps more fulfilling than the journey itself. Every success builds self-esteem, which in turn, boosts your confidence and courage.

If you can do something once, then you can do it again. Taking action, even if you find it difficult, helps you grow. It enables you to live the life you're meant to live.

Those who don't take risks, big or small, may find themselves living wistfully about a future that will never arrive. They may wish they had taken opportunities when they had the chance. Consider this: if time and circumstance pass you by, will you feel as though you have been left out or that you missed out on your chance?

Many people have a sense that they don't want to look back at 70 or 80 years of age, wishing that somehow their lives had been different.

Ask yourself:

- What would happen if I did this one thing?
- What would happen if I didn't do anything?

Make a list of the things that scare you the most. Rank each event on a scale of 1-10, with 10 being the highest

regarding scariness. Now find the one with the lowest *"fear factor"* score.
What would it take for you to do it?

Choosing satisfaction and wanting more

According to a *2016 Gallup Poll*, some of the happiest people in the world live in Sweden and Brazil. Their feelings are based on their sense of well-being, which comes from their health and wealth. The four dimensions come into play here: the physical, intellectual, emotional and spiritual cornerstones. Satisfaction is based on the perception of meeting the needs in these dimensions.

Happiness and the satisfaction that comes from it can be fleeting, however. Changes in health care options, income sources and living conditions can alter perception and feelings of contentedness. All of these are material. It's not the things in life that matter. Our connection to others is what matters most.

You can take charge of your own happiness and measure your own levels of satisfaction by looking at your **PSP Circle**: your personal, social, and professional relationships.

The PSP Circle

Imagine a series of concentric rings. Each slightly smaller ring sits within another.

The tiniest ring at the center of everything is the personal circle. This circle represents the relationships you have with your spouse or partner, your family, and your closest friends. Even though this circle may be the smallest, it is perhaps the most significant in your PSP Circle. For many people, this is the nucleus of their well-being. The personal circle is the heart of everything. It is here that they discuss their hopes and dreams, try on new ideas, and look to for validation.

A weak personal circle may leave you feeling adrift, but a strong one will bolster your self-esteem and confidence.

The next ring in the PSP Circle is your social circle. This ring includes your casual friendships and acquaintances, like the neighbors you see occasionally. Many people find that this circle easily consists of three hundred or more contacts. You may think that's a huge number, but look at your social media pages. How many contacts do you have? How many contacts are listed in your phone? And finally, how many more people do you know that are not listed in your contacts, like the coffee barista or the young man who checks in your dry cleaning?

Add more acquaintances, and your ring increases, giving you the social capital you need to strengthen the circles before and after this one. Some of these acquaintances could become close friends, and some could become colleagues.

The third ring is your professional circle. It is here that you find your co-workers and colleagues as well as your supervisors and bosses. In most cases, they are part of the largest part of your week. When you take successful risks at work, your efforts are usually rewarded with some sort of recognition. Successful risk-taking widens your professional circle, giving you authority and making you an influencer in your field.

As this circle widens, you'll also increase the size of your social circle, and that will affect your personal circle as well.

No single ring in the PSP circle exists in isolation. The circles are always moving fluidly. The rings cannot be isolated because relationships are dependent on each other. Each ring ripples against the other, influencing its movement in a liquid dance that sways back and forth. For that reason, the best relationships are developed not in isolation but rather, in synergy.

Every relationship is dependent on those nearby. So how do you create great relationships and keep them in motion?

You run each of them through a filter that aligns with your moral compass. Remember your four dimensions of physical, intellectual, emotional and spiritual strength? These cornerstones are also the measure of who you should have in each of these circles.

As you sift relationships through your filters, determine which you hold most dearly. Then look for similar-minded people. If you value daily exercise, spend more time with those who exercise. If the pursuit of higher education attracts you, allow those with similar interests into your professional, social, and even your personal circle.

What you hold most dear is what you will spend the most time on. All you have to do is surround yourself with like-minded people who feel the same way. Include them in the ripples of your life.

It is equally critical that you avoid the crabs in your life. These are the people who want to hold you back from achieving the kind of success you deserve. They are like crabs, their claws clicking at you and pulling you downward. That's what crabs do, especially if they're all in the same bucket. As soon as one crab (you!) climbs to the rim of the bucket, poised to move on to bigger things, another crab will come along and pull you back into the bucket again.

Anyone who goes crabbing knows that there is no need to put a lid on the bucket of crabs to hold them back. The crabs do it all by themselves.

There are people in your life like that. They want to hold you back, and whether consciously or unconsciously, they intend to prevent you from reaching your next level of success or freedom.

The woman who is victimized by an abuser finds herself in this situation. So does the child or the adult tormented by bullies. They are unable to grow and expand their PSP Circles because of the crabs nipping at their heels.

If you are in this situation, it's time to dump the crabs and develop new circles of friends and colleagues.

Failure to thrive or the will to live

Taking a risk is never easy. It's one of the scariest things you'll ever do. The one thing that holds many people back from effecting change in their lives is the fear of failure. Most people who think about making a change in their lives can run a long list of *"what ifs."*

The list often looks something like this. What if:

- I run out of money
- My health fails?

- I make a fool out of myself?
- I don't have the time?
- Others think poorly of me?
- My friends or coworkers won't be supportive?

You probably could add plenty of additional concerns to the list. In spite of all the questions you can think of about failing, you're forgetting the most important question of all:

What if you don't fail?

Healthy relationships and good habits are seldom convenient. They are something you work at, and that takes commitment on your part. Real work. But if you keep at it, the rewards speak for themselves. People ready to help you keep your self-esteem buoyed will surround you and lift you up.

Do more than live – thrive!

The motivation to do well is based on **taking action**. If you seek the motivation to make a change, you *must* act. You have to move forward. No change comes from inertia. Inactivity is the easier option, but it will hold you back.

It sounds simple. Just put one foot in front of the other and move forward, right? If it were that easy, you would have already take the steps you needed.

What's holding any of us back? For some of us, it's self-doubt, which in turn, eats into our self-esteem. That negative voice in our head whispers that we're not smart enough, good enough, rich enough, healthy enough, thin enough . . . . **Enough!**

If you let it, the negative voice will bind your feet and squash your dreams. No matter how that that voice gets – and it can really shout at you – you can turn in back down. First, ask the voice, *"How true is that statement, really?"*

If your negative voice tells you can't ask for a raise at work, respond with, *"How true is that?"* Or ask, *"Why?"* Make sure you ask an open-ended question – one that can't be answered with a yes or no question. An open-ended response requires thought and discourse. That's exactly what you want to produce a conversation with yourself.

When your inner voice says, *"Oh you can't ask for that raise?",* counter, with *"Why not?"*

Imagine the rest of the conversation going like this:

VOICE: Because you won't get it.
YOU: Says who?

VOICE: Says me. You're never right about anything.
YOU: Not true. I've been right before.

VOICE: What if you ask and don't get it?
YOU: What if I ask and do get it? Then who wins?

Many scenarios can play out when you confront your inner critic. With practice, you'll find that you can silence the voice that squashes self-esteem and saps your confidence. In the chapters ahead, we'll walk through several scenarios with varying outcomes, and you'll learn how to turn the negative voice into an ally that can assist you in moving forward.

In the meantime, if self-coaching doesn't get you moving, you might consider working with a professional coach who will use similar techniques to help you quiet the naysayer's voice and let you take the kind of action that will boost your self-esteem.

The sooner you take your first steps, the better. Delays feed the negative voice, giving it more strength to force you into stasis and decline. That's where negativity and a failure to thrive take root and pull you down into the doldrums.

By committing to take action, you have initiated the motivation process. You are moving forward – and that's something to be proud of.

As you take action, remember to include your PSP circle. Those in your family & friends and social circles share many of the same values. You've hand-picked these people to be your support. They're likely going to agree that you've worked and deserve that raise. Those people in your professional circle will second that.

Remember that a single link in a chain is useless by itself. It must connect with and work in conjunction with the other links in the chain.

Sometimes a link will break. Hope will fail you. Maybe you knew would happen eventually, or maybe you just didn't see it coming. You will feel like giving up, but there are ways to mend the chain. You can either repair the link or forge a new one.

The deciding factor that leads to success is whether or not you're willing to mend or move on. Your decision will be based on two things:

- How badly do you want it?
- What happens if you don't get it?

Winston Churchill offered insight on how to figure out whether you should pursue your goal or let it go: *"Never give up on something you can't go a day without thinking about."*

How To Stop Giving Up

If you are ready to commit to the things in life that matter most to you, you'll overcome any obstacles in front of you. Giving up won't be an option.
You'll also release yourself from your past to gain more confidence in future. Courage is not an abandonment of reason and good judgment. Courage is your secret weapon when it comes to asserting yourself. Courage is what happens when you know you are nervous and scared, but you do it anyway.

There's no chest-beating bravado in confidence. It's more about agonizing through the twisted stomach knots and cold sweats you have when thinking about your next steps. Here are just a few of the physiological responses you can expect: lightheadedness, clammy palms, tingling in your fingers and toes, and a tummy that wants to jump into your mouth. That's normal. The emotions you may feel range from nervousness to outright fear, but they will drive you to take action.

Courage is about caring enough to make a change. You are worth the care and effort it takes to create and endure change. If you can care enough to commit, you will find an increase in your self-esteem and your confidence. After all, as the Chinese philosopher Lao Tzu said, *"From caring comes courage."*

And with courage, you will be unstoppable. To get there, you have to dump the what Ifs and make the jump.

You have to do the one thing that scares you the most, whether that's fear of air travel or having a conversation with your boss. Do it by being present, positive, and productive:

Be present. You cannot change the past. You only can change your actions in the present, and that will have the greatest effect on your future.

Be positive. Find the good in every scenario, no matter how bad the situation. Knowing that there is something positive will give you hope.

Be productive. Ask yourself, *"What one thing can I accomplish today?"* Make a list if need be, but keep in mind that lists can quickly become overwhelming.

Most people will try to take the easiest path. You could do the same thing, but you won't grow, you won't change, and it's far less likely that you'll achieve your dreams. Playing it safe isn't playing it well at all.

Developing Courage and Confidence

Kids and confidence

Kids can be amazing. They make up goals and then try to achieve them. A lot of the time, children are successful, too. They don't know they can't, so they can. Of course, it takes plenty of encouragement along the way. They need adults in their lives who cheer them on and make risk-taking rewarding.

That changes when we become adults. Somewhere along the way, we discover more than a few things that we actually can't do, and as a result, our confidence takes a hit. No amount of encouragement is going to help us. Too often we mistake encouragement for confidence. We act as if encouraging someone will help make them confident. It doesn't.

The reverse is true. Confidence comes first. Demonstrate the first signs of confidence, and then you begin to receive encouragement. Pep talks are more effective when based on an action, no matter how small. Action produces encouragement.

So where does confidence come from? It comes from the small stuff, like learning how to do something for yourself. After all, success breeds more success. Children learn to hold a spoon, drink from a cup, and tie their shoes. Every milestone, regardless of how small, is one more chink in their armor of confidence. Kids know that if they can be successful at one thing, they may well be just as successful, if not more successful, at the next thing.

In the last chapter, we talked about being present, positive, and productive. Many children have mastered these skills.

They live in the present because they have a short past. When you're young, it's hard to see your future. It's hard to wait until your next birthday, much less imagine what you'll be like when you read the old age of twenty-five or more!

Generally speaking, children tend to have a positive outlook unless they've experienced a traumatic event. That doesn't mean that kids are always happy. It means that they understand that even though there may be difficult times, there will good times, too. Positive kids raised well know that their world isn't all or nothing. Nothing is ever all bad or all good, but they hold onto hope as they look for the good.

There's a story that illustrates this concept.

Six-year-old Patty wanted a pony more than anything in the world. Every birthday and every Christmas, she waited with anticipation for the one gift that would make her dreams come true. In the meantime, Patty played with toy horses, decorated her room with pictures of horses, and she talked about horses, non-stop. Her parents grew more than a little concerned about Patty's obsession, so they took her to a psychologist. The shrink took Patty into a room containing only two things: horse manure and a shovel. Patty's eyes widened, and she ran excitedly into the room, where she immediately began shoveling.

When asked what she was doing, Patty replied: *"With this much horse poo, I just know my pony has to be here somewhere!"*

Here's the other thing about children. If you've spent any time with kids, you know they are doers. In the course of a single day, they may attend school, go to practice, eat meals, play with friends, tease siblings, feed the family pet, play outside, play on their phone, draw a picture, and read a book. They are productive and always into something. Kids like to be busy; it's in their nature. If you don't find something for them to do, they'll find it on their own.

So why is it so hard to be like a kid?

For one thing, adults have different responsibilities than children. You have a job and maybe a family. There are utilities and food to pay for, clothing to wash, and plenty of obligations that need your constant attention. Many of the things you do, you do for others, not for yourself. How many of the things on your to-do list are for you? You are productive, but perhaps not in the carefree way you were when you were a child.

What would your life be like if you could recapture the active nature of your childhood once again?

To experience that child-like productivity, schedule play time for yourself. Try setting aside at least 30 minutes a week of *"free play"* time. Refrain from selecting the activity beforehand. Wait until the moment arrives, and then use the time however you want. Be curious. Be spontaneous. Avoid judgment. You may rediscover your creativity and even a youthful joy during this special time.

As you've matured, you've also gathered a variety of experiences along your journey. Some of these experiences have been good, and others you might have enjoyed less. All the same, they are your experiences, and they make you the person you are now. Because of them, you've developed a filter for everything that happens. The filter is woven from the threads of every past event, good or bad, and you use this filter to evaluate what's happening to you every moment that you feel an emotion.

Like Patty, it's up to you to find decide whether your response will be positive or negative.

Check on your reactions with regularity. Some people like to end their day by reflecting on the positives of the day. The process is similar to writing a gratitude journal, where you identify one thing you're grateful for each day. In a positivity journal, however, you list the positives you discovered: new blooms on your begonia, someone doing something nice for you, no bills in today's mail – anything thing that's a positive in your life.

Encourage your inner child to pick out the positives from your day. The caveat here is that you must identify what's a positive for you, not for someone else. If you love rainstorms, but your partner or spouse doesn't, and an afternoon thunderstorm boomed all around you and rattled the windows, count it as a positive. It's your positivity journal, not theirs.

Some people like looking for positives throughout the day. That may mean starting your day by identifying what's right with the world and checking in with yourself with each change of state. You finished a meeting? What went well? You embarked on a new project? What's the best part about it? Every positive is one more piece of confidence that helps to build your courage.

Looking for the best in the people and situations we encounter helps us see how much good there is all around us.

Children approach life with a naiveté that's refreshing. They rarely have preconceived ideas. By living in the present, they seem to have plenty of time to enjoy themselves. Best of all, they trust. It's that faith that gives them confidence, even when something terrible happens. Because you've celebrated plenty of positives, your confidence will carry you beyond the negatives.

You can still recapture some of that youthful confidence for yourself. Be present in everything you do. If you're having a conversation at work or with a friend, avoid the temptation to check your social media. Give yourself permission to enjoy a little free time each week. It doesn't have to be planned; it just has to be yours. Find what's positive, and focus on that.

Most of all, trust yourself, the way you did when you were a kid. All it takes is a little courage, and that's what you've been building up for yourself.

6 Acts of Courage

Courage means facing your fear and doing it anyway, but as it turns out, that's easier said than done.

Building up your courage is like snowboarding. The sport is based on conditions, technology, and skill. You need the right amount of snow, and it helps if it's not too slushy, but not too hard-packed either. Then there's gear you need: boards, bindings, gloves, goggles, and more. Finally, the best rippers practice. They try out their skill in a variety of conditions, so they are ready for anything.

To increase your confidence to the point that you are courageous, practice your skills in a variety of conditions and with the right gear. You can hone your courage by engaging in these six acts of courage.

Dreams are what carry us forward

Without them, it's hard to move beyond where you are now. Think about it. Your dreams of your future are what have gotten you where you are now. You set out to do something in exchange for achieving a goal. That may mean you attended a university or worked at a particular job until you found your real path. Maybe you're still looking for that path. Either way, it's likely that you had to delay gratification, if even for a bit, to pursue your dream.

What about someone with no dreams? Without dreams, a person has nothing to look forward to. There's nothing to work toward and little with which to increase your confidence. Dreaming is about identifying goals. That's something everyone can do. It's costs nothing but means everything. The secret to dreaming lies in being specific about what you want.

It's not enough to say, *"I'd like to be my own boss"* or *"I want to be rich."*

You've got to say, *"I want to earn one million dollars by the time I'm 30."* Use your own numbers. Being more specific in setting goals can help you achieve them. Specific goals have milestones. Every milestone you can tick off the list helps you to reach your goals. In turn, you are making your dreams come true. Best of all, you are building up your self-esteem and confidence each time you check off something specific.

To be your own boss, for example, you need a plan. Define what being a boss looks like. Are you the sole employee in your business? Do you want to hire people? Or is passive income your thing? If you can articulate what being your own boss means to you, you are on your way to picturing your dream.

Once you know what you want to do, it's easy enough to build a plan to make it happen. You can follow the paths of others, or get help.

It's harder to make it happen, though. Plans are only plans until they are put into action. If you let them gather dust, you're no farther along than if you had done nothing. A plan becomes a strategy when you commit to action. Many a dreamer has said they felt like throwing in the towel and giving up. Making a dream come true takes hard work, and it helps to have a mentor or coach who can help you stay on track.

Face Reality

Facing reality is a necessary part of developing courage. Doing it can be unpleasant. Reality is sometimes ugly, with warts and bristly hairs. Scary.

That may mean taking a deep breath and doing the little things you hate to do, like opening bills you know you can't pay or listening to your kid's teacher complain about how your child got in trouble again. Facing reality is also owning up to situations you may have caused, like that fender-bender last week.

Reality is recognizing that you have a dead-end job. It's admitting that you have unhealthy behaviors or that your relationships with others need work. No one like to hear negative comments, especially when it's the truth. It hurts. But you can take that hurt and change your life if you're willing to see the situation for what it is. It's not until we can face reality that we can do something about it. See the truth for what it is, and remember that just because it is true now, it doesn't have to be true forever. By identifying your reality, you can decide whether to keep it or change it. That's where courage comes in. You may feel afraid, but you do it anyway.

Confront & Be Confronted

Most people don't like conflict. They try to avoid it, and they'll go to great lengths to stay away from dust-ups and skirmishes. Some people would rather give up than speak up. Confrontation doesn't have to be aggressive, violent, or even mean. Although it can be fraught with negative connotations, confrontation is about identifying a challenge (facing reality) and doing something about it.

It's likely that you have multiple opportunities to confront and be confronted throughout your day. When the waiter brings you a well-done steak even though you ordered it rare, what do you do? Some people will saw through the meat and arduously chew every bite, saying nothing. They want to avoid confrontation.

Others figure, I'm paying for this steak, so I want it cooked according to my tastes. They'll send the steak back because it's not right. How the steak gets sent back is another thing altogether. You can choose to sling the beef across the restaurant at the waiter or handle the confrontation more respectfully. Simply say, *"I order my steak rare, and this appears well-done. I'd like the order corrected."*

You're still confronting someone about a less than ideal situation. The difference is that you are doing it with a neutral face and calm voice. You're matter-of-fact. *Calm. Professional. Confident.*

There are times that you will be the one confronted. Someone may have a simple concern or a serious complaint that you will have to hear out. Begin the same way you confront someone else. Keep your face as neutral as possible, and most importantly, listen. Let the other person say what they need to say without interrupting them. When it's your turn, respond with the same neutral face and calm voice you use for confronting others. Think of confrontation as an engagement rather than a battle. Learning how to engage and speak up for yourself can build your confidence and fill you with courage.

Learn & Grow

The one constant in life is change. We can count on nothing ever remaining the same.

Ten years ago many people insisted they'd never be so busy that they would need to carry a mobile phone. Now they not only have a mobile phone, but they have also canceled their landline services. They rely exclusively on the one device they take everywhere with them – even to bed.

Attitudes change, too. The food you used to love may no longer taste as good to you. You probably don't wear the same clothing style you wore ten years ago or even three years ago. Relationships also change. They deepen and grow stronger, or they dissipate and fade away.

You can prepare for change by preparing yourself for the inevitable. That means learning and growing. Some people find they must unlearn some things. Five hundred years ago people discovered that the world is round, not flat. Today, we know that cigarette smoke is harmful, and Pluto is no longer a planet. As you improve your knowledge of the how the world works and your skills to deal with it, you also become more receptive to future change. To learn how to accept imminent change, you have to educate yourself. Education comes in many forms. It can be formal or informal, and either type can be customized to your unique needs.

Some people opt for formal education by enrolling in a university to earn one or more degrees. Formal education can also include adding professional certificates to your name. For example, you may choose to specialize in an area beyond your major and minor areas of study, and that certificate may make you more marketable.

Informal education can also help you be more marketable. It does something else for you, too. It broadens your horizons and gives you a sense of fulfillment. It creates confidence, and it elevates self-esteem. Learning and growing can make you happy.

If you've always wanted to learn to paint or weld, take a community class. Do you love history? Try out an online course; many colleges offer non-credit courses for free. You can even Google a hobby you're curious about. Watch a few YouTube videos and try your hand at the new skill.

Whatever you choose, remember that you're also building confidence by learning a new skill. It's possible that you'll discover that you love what you're learning. And if you don't? Let it go and move on. It's the experience that counts. The important thing is that you tried.

You were willing to try something new. To explore change, perhaps even to embrace it. Learning and growing shapes you into a well-rounded person. In essence, when you are willing to learn and grow, you too are changing, keeping up with the times. You may like what you find there.

Be Vulnerable

There's a woman in our book club who embraces vulnerability. She is unafraid to show her emotions, and she has a lot of them. When a character she's reading about experiences sadness and loss, she's not afraid to cry. In fact, her tears come easily any time something triggers her emotions. She hates the fact that she cries so easily, but her vulnerability is endearing.

Vulnerability makes her human. It also makes her approachable. As it turns out, though, we're taught to be strong, not vulnerable. Never let them see you cry, we're told. Showing emotion and being vulnerable is seen as a sign of weakness. To be vulnerable is to lose your position of power, according to some.

In reality, vulnerability gives you authenticity. When you allow yourself to be vulnerable, you are being realistic. Most importantly, you are being true to yourself rather than someone others want you to be. You learn to be honest. You'll also become the best version of yourself. When you can accept yourself for who you really are, you are in a position of power.

Take Action

The final act of courage comes in the form of action. All of the dreams and vulnerability in the world will do you no good unless you're willing to take action. Dreams are only dreams unless you convert them into goals and take the steps to make them happen. Facing reality requires that act. So does confronting and being confronted. Learning and growing, accepting your vulnerability – it all takes action on your part.

Refusing to engage creates isolation, and a lack of commitment causes depression. By avoiding action, you are setting yourself up for failure. You may find yourself living a life that is far less than what you deserve. You are cheating yourself and those around out of being the person you were destined to be.

Taking action can be frightening. It's like stepping off the platform and jumping into the air, with nothing connecting you to your past but a bungee cord. Going away to school can feel the same way. So can buying a home or even changing your hairstyle. Taking action is what will help you grow into who want to be. The more you do for yourself, the more confidence you will build up, and that confidence produces courage.

Fake It 'til You Make It

How often have you been told to *"fake it until you make it?"* Sometimes that's exactly the advice you need. Other times, it won't be your best bet.

Focusing too much on faking it until you make it can catapult you into a contest you'll never win. You know the fake it until you make it type that tries too hard. She's the woman who follows the latest beauty and fashion trends in the hopes that she'll be accepted with the right group of friends. He's the one who purchased the expensive sports car so that others - coworkers, the boss, a girlfriend - will notice him.

We recommend not faking it until you make unless you can afford the lifestyle change you are about to embrace, and unless you fake it for the right reasons. Drowning in debt won't make you feel like a champ. It will make you feel inadequate and overwhelmed. It will eat at your confidence. You'll spend your efforts on keeping up rather than getting ahead. Make the real focus on your transformation into a more authentic and confident version of yourself.

Get yourself there your honest answer to one question: *"Who am I doing this for?"*

If you're wearing an expensive watch because you like it, you may be on the right track. The same is true of a high-maintenance hairstyle or living in an expensive home. If, however, you're wearing that same watch or flashing any other status symbol in the hopes that someone else will like you, you're doing it for the wrong reason. When proving your value to others consumes you, it's time to stop faking it. You may be endangering your health, your finances, and even your future. Relentless devotion to appearances comes across as superficial and shallow. It's a shell that encases low-self-esteem.

Adopting affected behaviors and affluent material objects won't magically turn you into the person you want to become. Your change will be hollow. The very people you want to impress will see how hard you're trying. They'll also see through your actions, regardless of how well-meaning they are. So how does anyone pull it off? Begin by identifying what it is you need to do.

For example, if you want others to see you as management material, define what makes a manager in your industry. Do your research, talk to influencers, and make a list. Include every facet you can think of. What level of education is required? What about experience? Consider how the leaders and influencers in your industry dress and act.

Imitate their actions. Stay within your means, but think outside your box. If you want to become the kind of leader who communicates well, consider joining a Toastmasters group to work on your communication and leadership skills. Find a mentor who will guide you, give you advice and cheer you on. Keep your social media current and professional, or hire someone to do it for you. Start your metamorphosis by faking it until you make it.

But what if your only goal is to be more confident as you go about your everyday business? Apply the same strategy. What is it that confident people do that you also want to do? Select the one or two characteristics you want to practice. Find networking opportunities by joining a group that has interests similar to yours. Connect with a mentor who will help you on your journey. Maintain your positive social media connections. You'll be faking it until you make it, but more importantly, you'll be adopting the routines and habits of the highly confident.

Faking it until you make it can help you create meaningful change. You might not be a morning person, but by getting up at 5:00 a.m. every day, you discover how much you can get done before everyone gets up and starts their day. By practicing your smile on a regular basis, you may discover something amazing. You're more positive throughout the day. People enjoy being around you. The positive attitude that a smile can generate is contagious. It makes a difference in not only your day but in that of everyone around you as well.

After you adopt the first strategies in your transformation, continue adding both new characteristics and mind power techniques that will move you toward improved self-esteem and confidence.

How To Easily Harness The Power Of Your Mind

Your mind is the most powerful tool in your arsenal when it comes to developing self-esteem and confidence. Your mind can help you address your negative thoughts and turn them into positive ones. You can teach your brain to reframe situations, believe in yourself, create passion, and to develop a resolve to achieve your goals and dreams. Sound impossible?

If you use the right visualization and reframing techniques, anything is possible.

Affirmations

Every day you make hundreds if not thousands of decisions. Some of them will have a significant impact, and others are not so important. Every time you do make a decision, you commit to either action or non-action. Every action or non-action affords you with the opportunity to evaluate not only the outcome but especially yourself. If you revert to negative and abusive self-talk, you risk chipping away at the self-esteem you've been building up.

Rather than let voices of doubt shred your progress, squelch them early on by affirming what's good and right. You could spend your time worrying about what you should have done or said, but instead, affirm what went well, using the skills already taught here.

Tell yourself, *"I may have woken up thirty minutes late, but I was only five minutes late to work"* or *"I'm making progress toward my goals."*

Celebrate every win, no matter how small.

Catabolic Bingo

Sometimes negativity and anxiety won't go away. They're persistent pests, consistently nagging at your thoughts. You're so busy trying to swat them away that you don't have time for much else. They are consuming your day – and sometimes your nights, as well. The catabolic energy eats at your self-esteem and shreds your confidence, making it hard to be courageous.

Try Catabolic Bingo, a strategy that lets you embrace problems head-on. You play it by identifying your pet peeves. Make yourself a bingo card. Pick the size of your card, but try not to have more than twenty-five squares. If you do have more than twenty-five pet peeves, play two (or three) cards simultaneously. Create cards with any more than twenty-five squares, and you may have problems filling out your card.

Write one pet peeve in each square. These irritations can be as small or large as you'd like. For example, if you frequently get stuck in traffic, write that down. If your mobile phone battery drains too quickly, Write it in a square, too. Mosquitoes or spiders? Write it in a square. Anything that annoys you goes into one of your bingo squares.

When you fill your card completely, you're ready to play. Every time one of your pet peeves happens, and it will, mark it on the square. You can even write the date or the time if you like. When you complete a horizontal, vertical or diagonal row, you've won the game.

You can decide how you want to reward yourself for your bingo, but the real prize lies in analyzing why these irritations matter so much to you. For example, are your pet peeves things you can control, or are they beyond your control?

You may not be able to control traffic, but you can control your reaction to it. When you notice that this square comes up frequently in your catabolic bingo games, it's time to make a change. Take a different route or leave earlier or later to avoid getting stuck in traffic. If your mobile phone battery constantly needs changing, make a plan to recharge your phone consistently or buy a new battery.

The thing about playing Catabolic Bingo with yourself is that you will tire of it. As you do, you'll find yourself either making changes so irritations no longer bother you or you'll wonder why the issue bothered you in the first place. You will tire of the petty pet peeves taking up so much of your day.

In either case, you've taught yourself to move on.

Reframing

Home designers and house flippers do it all the time. They take a dated property and reframe it. They change the look, redefine the style and improve perception. You can do the same thing when you want to build your self-esteem. Reframe the situation.

Here's how it works:

If your spouse or partner asks what time will you be home from work, your first response may be, *"Why?"* Instead of being defensive, consider that the other person may want to include you in plans or may be concerned for your safety. Rather taking offense that your boss wants to see your work before you finish it, reframe the situation by looking for why your boss wants to do this. Is it micro-manage you or to guide your through the project?

You can help others with reframing, too:

If your teenager hates that you are always checking his or her grades, help your child understand the reason for doing it. You are checking grades because you love your child and want his or her success.

To reframe a situation, take yourself out of the picture completely. Imagine that you are standing on the outside, looking through a picture window at the scene. What do you see? Who are the players? What is their motive?

Reframing helps you see the present with new eyes. You are less likely to react as a victim who asks, *"Why me?"* and you will be more likely to become conscious of differing or alternative opinions.

These opinions are neither bad or good; they simply differ from yours. You can choose whether to agree or disagree with them, but when you do, you'll be coming from a place of confidence.

Visualizing

Visualizing is a technique similar to reframing, but instead of focusing on the present, visualizing looks to the future. You can use the same picture frame or window for visualizations. For this technique, you imagine your future.

If your journey to improved self-esteem has meant losing weight, imagine how you will look when you achieve your goal. Pretend that you are seeing yourself as others see you. How does it feel to weigh less? Imagine yourself going through the motions as your new self. See yourself in the new body and imagine how it feels to move around in it.

You can visualize almost anything. Imagine yourself working in a job you love. What hours are you working? What is the environment like? What kind of benefits do you have? What's your salary? Take yourself through an entire day in your new profession, from the moment you walk in the door until you leave at the end of the day.

Visualization is similar to faking it until you make it. It sets the vision for where you want to be and what you want to become. Athletes use this technique before big games. They visualize every movement in their performance, right down to their contact with the ball or the feel of the ice skate blade on the ice.

Artists do the same thing. When asked about his process for creating sculptures, Michaelangelo once said that he carved stone to set an angel free. He had seen the image in the marble, and his visualization produced the art that became St. Michael the Archangel. Your ability to visualize your future will produce your reality.

Try this right now. Close your eyes. Think about a person who demonstrates self-esteem. What does that look like? Observe what the person is doing. What actions show confidence? Notice what the person is wearing. What are they saying? Now imagine that the person you see before you is changing. He or she is beginning to look more like you. You are doing and saying things with confidence. You look confident. You are filling yourself with self-esteem, and you are becoming more and more confident. Visualize yourself as that courageous person.

Self-beliefs and assumptions

What we believe isn't always what's right or true. The truth can be elusive. That's because we create assumptions and then abide by them.

An assumption can be something simple. You go to lunch with a colleague who always orders water and a small side salad, although everyone else orders a large meal. You may assume that this person isn't hungry or doesn't have the money for an entrée. Without asking for the reason, you may have made an erroneous judgment about your colleague's decision.

By talking with the person, you may discover that the real reason for the small salad is that your colleague doesn't like to eat a large lunch. It's not their favorite meal of the day. Assumptions about self-esteem and confidence work the same way.

If you've made a conjecture about yourself, you may be sabotaging your self-esteem. For example, by telling yourself, diets never work for me, you're making an assumption that will extinguish your chances of success. Instead of assuming that a new diet won't work, challenge it. What about the diet will work? Look for facts, not opinions.

Accepting assumptions at face value means you're missing out on vital information. Asking if something is true or valid can help you abolish assumptions.

Creating passion, desire and resolve

People who have a passion for something are more likely to develop confidence. That's because they put time, money, and effort into doing what they love. The more time they spend doing what they love, the more they increase their skills and their overall sense of satisfaction. You may be wondering, how do I get some of that?

Identify what you love most. What is the non-negotiable in your life? What can you not live without? For some people, that be a hobby like woodworking or jewelry-making. It may be a pastime like golf, fishing, or reading. Give yourself permission to do what you love because by spending time doing what you love, you're investing in your self-esteem and building confidence.

Likes/Dislikes Exercise

What if you don't have anything you love doing? It's time to try this exercise. Grab a piece of paper and divide the page in half. On one half of the paper, write Likes. On the other half, write Dislikes.

Start making lists. What are some things you find pleasant? They can be as personal or general as you feel comfortable writing about. Get them written down.

Work on your dislikes, too. By identifying what you do not like doing, you free your mind to think about what it would prefer to do instead. Hate dusting? Write it down. Hate folding clothes or mowing your lawn? Write those down, too. Then think about what you'd rather be doing, and go back to listing what you like.

Now looks at your list of likes. What stands out to you? Circle the two or three things that call to you. That's your sweet spot. When you find what you like, you're ready to take action and make it happen. That's where you'll find more of your confidence.

The One Question You Must Ask Yourself

As you transform yourself into a person with more confidence, you have the opportunity to redefine yourself completely and become who you want to be. You can change not only what you think but also how you respond to your thoughts.

The one question you must ask yourself is, *"Who am I?"* Answering the question will take both analysis and visioning.

Let's begin with the analysis: **Who are you?**

Think about what you believe in and what you stand for. For some people, it's their faith or their family. It may be their work or involvement with others. Take a few minutes now to think about what is most important to you?

For this visualization part, who do you want to be? If you could be the best version of yourself possible, what would that look like? Consider not just how you look, but what your thoughts, actions, and words would be. How will you make your visualization a reality?

By developing a personal mission statement, you create a philosophy by which to gauge any reaction to what's happening in your life. You can react with confidence because you have a code by which you live. Visualizing yourself doing it completes the process.

Emotions

Courage comes from confidence. You can build your confidence by using your emotions as a springboard for achieving the results you want.

As we've discussed before, your actions are the result of your thoughts, and your thoughts come from your emotions. Everyone experiences multiple emotions and even varying nuances of those emotions throughout their day. Emotions can make your feelings seem multifaceted, but they come down to two types: positive and the negative emotions.

Emotions can destroy, or they can launch you forward. Anxiety, for example, can destroy good health and bring about relationship issues. Remember Wendy, from the first chapter? Her anxiety ate away at her relationship with not only her husband, but also with her boss. She compromised her health and possible her marriage and job. Love, on the other hand, is a positive emotion that inspires us to be better individuals. Wendy's husband can affirm his relationship with his wife through love. His likelihood of success depends on his and Wendy's reaction to how they each feel.

What's amazing about emotions is that we can control how we respond to them. Regardless of what we feel, we can determine the way in which we'll respond to the emotion we experience.

Baggage or Buoys

Crippling emotions that weigh us down harm self-esteem and obliterate confidence. It's nearly impossible to find courage at this point; even survival can be tough. The negative emotions are like a confining net that tangles your efforts to swim to the top for air.

Negative emotions bring about destruction. They tear up relationships and cause resentment. They favor inaction.

The Dali Lama says that only two things that cause these negative emotions of destruction. Focusing on appearances and being self-centered will cause the most significant harm.

Those who worry the most about appearances are living in falsehood. They have concentrated their focus more on how they look in the eyes of everyone else, rather than focusing on their inner selves. The external is less important than the internal because it is who you are on the inside that matters most.

If you let them, your emotions will force you to focus on appearances. That why it's so critical that you stop negative emotions in their tracks. You can use emotions like anger and fear to bring about positive change.

People who are self-centered may or may not be focused on their appearances, but they always look out for themselves first. Wondering what's in it for me or playing the victim creates discord and sows the seed of low-self-esteem. By accepting either role, the self-centered person often trades their confidence for contempt.

Don't let your emotions have the power to cripple you. You have the strength you need to decide if your emotions will be baggage or buoys. With practice, you can overcome any emotion you're feeling and use it to your advantage to live courageously and with confidence. Here's how.

Anger

Anger is one of the most volatile emotions that humans experience. It's the fire of all emotion, burning deep within. If you can harness it, you use it to fuel your goals, but anger is every bit as dangerous as fire because it prompts the most physical of reactions.

The next time you feel angry, pinpoint exactly what made you feel this way. Because anger is so *"in the moment,"* you may have to reflect on this emotion after it has passed. Is it a person who made you mad or is it what the person did? Is it a situation? Could it have been prevented? How so? Carefully unravel each thread and analyze it for ways in which you can alter your reactions. By understanding precisely what it is that has angered you, you can move beyond the anger and make a change.

For example, if someone in the parking lot dents your car, you're probably furious about the dent. After all, it's your car, and you take good care of it – and now this has happened! Any person could have made the dent, not just the one standing in front of you. It would still be a dent, but dents can be repaired.

Shift your anger from the person who committed the offense to how you can take care of the repair. Look for the positive that will come from this, even if it means that at least you'll get your car washed.

Contempt

Contempt is judgment-based. The emotion you feel comes from a sense that someone or something has not met your expectations. Hatred encourages you to elevate yourself above everyone else, and it can make you self-centered. When you feel contempt for others, it's time to self-reflect. Ask yourself if you making a decision based on fact or on assumption. If you find yourself tied to assumptions, it may be time to get the facts before making your judgment.

Anyone can make assumptions, but they are based entirely on personal experience. They tend to be one-sided.

When you find yourself saying something negative (showing contempt) about another person, **stop**. Isolate what you said, and ask yourself how true the statement is.

When you see a mother with screaming toddlers at the supermarket, your first thought may be, *"What a terrible parent."* Stop, and consider why you chose the world terrible. Is she terrible? Do you know the entire situation? You may not know that the mom was up all night with two sick kids, and she's been to the doctor with them both but needed a few groceries before taking them home. You only know what you saw at the moment and made an assumption.

Let go. Let go of the contempt and avoid making assumptions. You'll find that it's healthier to either help the person in front of you or walk away without comment.

Disgust

Closely related to contempt, disgust also manifests from judgment, and it's based on assumption as well. It's hatred, the opposite of love. Disgust happens when you set a standard that others cannot or will not live up to. They may not even be aware of the standard you set, or it may be impossible for them to reach. When you experience such extreme hatred, ask yourself *why*.

Have you set an unreasonable standard? Have you created an expectation that the other person will never reach? Finally, decide if you can accept that person for who they are.

If so, great. If not, it may be time to move on.

Fear

No emotion grabs your attention like fear. There's a reason for that. Fear is one of the most useful feelings you can have because it helps you survive in two ways: safety and change. Fear stands out by itself because it can shut down your needs rather quickly. When you're afraid, your body won't feel hunger. It may not even feel pain.

When you feel afraid, your priority will be your safety. Fear will downshift you until you are operating in nearly primal mode, like first gear. Fear won't let you do or think about anything else until everything is okay again. You'll have to give yourself at least a few hours before exploring how your fear can help you makes changes.

Once your fear subsides, you can use the distress you felt to change your circumstances. That may mean driving to your vacation destination instead of flying, or it may mean leaving an abusive relationship. Fear makes you take action. You use fear to get yourself to a safe place.

Joy

As strange as it may seem to talk about using joy to advance your goals, joy is the one positive emotion most people want more of. Experiencing just the tiniest bit of happiness can have us yearning for more. We crave the endorphins that joy produces.

When you do experience joy, isolate the feeling. What is it that makes you feel blissful? Take careful inventory of your senses, noting what you see, feel, hear, smell, and taste.

Savor the moment, and visualize yourself in this state of complete enjoyment.

Your goal is to capture the essence of it so that you can pursue more of it. When you can recall joyfulness, you can take the kind of action that will allow you to experience it again and again.

Sadness

A bittersweet emotion, sadness can be painful, yet useful. Sadness gives us pause. It helps to slow us down and take time to reflect. Think about the many things that can cause sorrow. Losing a loved one makes us think about the time we had with the deceased. We reflect on actions. We think about the time we ourselves have left, and how precious that is.

When we are sorrowful, we are also vulnerable. It is here that we are the most approachable and willing to approach others – with humility and kindness. As the opposite of happiness, sadness helps us reflect and appreciate the better times in our lives. When you are sad, reflect on the cause. You may not be able to alter what has happened, but you can decide how you want to move forward. If your sorrow comes from loss, what's next for you? Is it time to renew a relationship, or do you need to reframe your own life?

Sadness can help move you to the next level of self-esteem and confidence. When sadness is the only emotion you experience, however, it may be time to consider getting professional help. Depression is a serious condition that may need professional intervention.

Surprise

Surprise keeps us alert and ready to respond. It's closely related to learning and growth, both of which are necessary for a fulfilling life. Wonder can bring delight, and it can help us make necessary changes in our lives. The problem with surprise is that most people don't appreciate being surprised. They fear not being competent in their reaction to it.

Learning how to enjoy surprise takes a high level of confidence, but if you've been practicing the techniques in this book, you'll find that you have the courage to face surprises head-on. Think of your emotions as stepping stones toward confidence and courage, not tombstones of low self-esteem. Be ready to embrace the change you'll experience.

Developing courage and confidence takes work. ***No one*** gets it right the first time. Every confident person can tell you about the time they failed. They took the fall, but they also started again. They gave it another try. The confident person keeps applying strategies that improve their self-esteem and live courageously.
You now have the tools to do the same.

Taking Action Now

If you've been practicing the techniques offered in this book, you're on your way to building up your self-esteem and becoming more confident but you must remember that increasing your self-esteem is a process. You can supercharge your confidence and have the courage you need for nearly any situation. Do it with intentional actions.

Confident body language and dress

One of the quickest ways to change not only the image you project but also your self-perception is through body language and dress. When you look good, you feel good, and when you feel good, your confidence soars. You can incorporate changes in body language, gestures and color immediately.

Body language says it all. It shows how you're feeling, whether you are a leader or a follower, and how you react. Your gestures and even your posture can make a difference in how you feel about yourself. As it turns out, your mom was right: stand up straight! Posture makes a difference in how others see you, and it affects how you see yourself as well. Good posture comes from standing straight, shoulders slightly back. Plant your feet slightly apart from each other, directly under your hips. Hold your head level and look forward.

Your sitting posture is just as important as your standing posture. Again, pull your spine upward. Sit with your buttocks planted square on the seat, and place both feet on the floor. Watch your posture, but check your actions as well. Constantly looking at your mobile phone signals that you're not interested or too nervous to talk with the people on your phone. It also affects your posture in either position. That's because the act of looking at your phone causes you to tilt your head downward and pull at least one shoulder forward – a position not conducive to confidence.

Slouching brings to mind all sorts of negative connotations: lazy, uneducated, aged, ill health, carelessness, passive. They're assumptions, of course, but they can hurt your image. Imagine creating the opposite effect by standing erect, with your shoulders back: competent, knowledgeable, healthy, active, hard worker. These too are assumptions, but which image would you rather create?

If you chose the positive one, you'll discover that you have more energy. It's actually more comfortable for your body to stand straight, with your shoulders back, arms relaxed, and knees slightly bent. Your skeleton, muscles, and ligaments want to be in alignment.

And what about your hands? Stuffing them in a pocket is a sign of nervousness or secrecy. Let your hands hang naturally from your wrist. They'll be in the right position if you'll shake your arms and wrists vigorously. Then let your arms and hands rest by your side, noticing how they feel in this position.

Your gestures also determine your self-esteem and confidence. Picture a person with arms crossed against the chest. What assumption do you make? If you're like most people, you assume that the person isn't open to sharing or socializing. Blocking communication, however, could be a sign of low self-esteem. People who gesture with their hands while talking should be careful that they don't engage in parallel hand and arm movements. Parallel movements occur when you simultaneously move your hands and arms in the same direction. Your gestures will be more effective, and you'll feel more confident if you execute a single movement at a time.

Another way to feel confident is to walk and talk at the same time. Simultaneously walking and talking increases your energy level and positivity. You'll appear confident and in charge, but pay careful attention to the kinds of conversations you're having. You'll discover that when they become serious or highly personal, you'll stop in your tracks to focus on the conversation.

Avoid pointing. This gesture indicates that you feel as though you are an authority figure and possibly superior to others. Rather than coming from a position of confidence, it suggests aggressiveness. Many cultures frown on this gesture, so it's best to not to use it at all. Instead, gesture with a single open hand.

Finally, *smile*. A sincere smile will energize the people around you, and you'll feel better, too. Smiling is one of the fastest and easiest ways to improve your self-esteem.

Using color as a confidence-booster

Extend your self-esteem boosting beyond body language. There are other techniques you can implement to improve self-esteem, and they take as much time to implement as it does to change your shirt. To build self-esteem fast, let the colors you wear do your talking.

Here's what your colors say about you:

Blue is social. It's also a calming color that promotes communication, especially if the shades you select lean toward aqua and turquoise. If you're attending a meeting where poise and confidence are critical, opt for navy blue. On a worldwide scale, many people prefer blue, so it's a good bet when you want to express intelligence, consistency, and calmness – all of which are part of positive self-esteem.

Wear **green** to connect with nature and feel peaceful. Shades of green are harmonious colors, and they will put you and others at ease. Light green is the color of new learning, fertility, and growth. The darker shades will make you feel connected to family and friends, like deep roots. Green suggests legacies, wealth, and tradition.

Your most significant boost in self-confidence comes from **yellow**. This color brings out inspiration and creativity, and it strengthens your positive emotions. The optimism that yellow generates can be contagious, so it's a great color to wear when you want others to enjoy having you around.

Orange is for risk-takers. It conveys images of excitement and success. Those people who willing to wear orange appear to be fascinating individuals who are fearless in personal expression and freedom. They find fun in the moment, and they embrace change. To rev up your adrenaline, try wearing any shade of orange and see what happens.

Red is a power color, both primal and intense. It's no secret that attorneys like their clients to wear read in court (the other favorite is navy). Red shrouds you in a shield of confidence like no other color. Leaders and celebrities like to wear red because this color makes them the focal point, which is a confident place to be. Sports teams favor red, and so does the military. Wear red when you want to feel invincible.

Purple suggests dignified royalty and wealth. It evokes a sense of mystery and eccentricity, and it can also promote creativity. Because it's related to red, purple denotes power and ambition. Tempered with blue, purple also means peace.

To be more confident, focus less on clothing styles and designers and more on the hue you choose to wear each day. Each color can have a positive effect on your outlook and confidence level, but be aware colors can also harbor negative connotations. It's up to you to decide how the color you choose will make you feel. You alone have the power to determine how color makes you feel. You may discover new strength in wearing colors that boost your confidence.

Eating and exercising your way to greater confidence

In the section discussing dimensions, we explored the physical, intellectual, emotional and spiritual dimensions. You learned about developing life-long habits that would elevate your self-esteem in each of these areas.

If you've been working on your physical dimension, you've made a conscientious effort to eat better and get regular exercise. Every day that you commit to your habit, you're getting closer to becoming the person you imagined yourself to be. Now, however, it's time for some fine-tuning.

First, review the types of foods you consume. Regardless of the diet plan you've selected for yourself, the quality of the food you eat is just as important as how much of it you consume. Ideally, your balance should include carbs (about half of your calories), protein (as much as one-third of your caloric intake), and fat should constitute about one-fifth of the food you eat. The numbers here don't add up to one hundred, because you must adjust the ratios based on your personal needs. To lose or gain weight, adjust the ratios based on your body type.

While it's true that the body also needs sugar and salt to perform well, be aware that these nutrients exist in some surprising places. The frozen chicken breast you buy can have as much as 600mg of salt in them. Most people need less than 2300mg of sodium per day. Colas and beverages that replace electrolytes contain nearly 40mg of sugar per serving; on average, adults need no more than 150mg of sugar daily.

As it turns out, too much sugar and salt may not be your only enemies. Consumers express concern about Genetically Modified Organisms (GMOs), fearing that they may increase organ damage. Nitrates in processed meats are another offender because of their link to cancer.

The more processing your food endures, it will be cheap, but less likely to be healthy. Unhealthy foods will make you feel awful, and this feeling will show in your levels of self-esteem. You may experience anxiety, nervousness, depression, irritability, all of which lower self-esteem.

Instead, eat foods closest to their natural state. Usually, these are the items at the perimeter of the grocery store. Most everything else on the shelves in the middle of the store is processed. Shop the perimeter for healthy foods, and you'll save money, too, because you're not paying for processing.

The next step is to ramp up your physical activity. You're probably exercising regularly thanks to your work in the physical dimension. The Mayo Clinic recommends logging 75 minutes of vigorous activity every week or 150 minutes of moderate activity. Either will produce lasting benefits, and best of all, you can chose both the exercise and the schedule of frequency that works best for you.

The important thing is that you do it. Skip a day, and only you will notice that you missed a session. Skip a week or more, and others will see a change in you. You'll see it, too, as you begin to lose your confidence. Never underestimate the effects of exercise/diet on confidence on the mind and body, or the importance of eating foods high in nutritional value. Your self-esteem, confidence, and well-being depend on it.

Powering up with emotions

Don't stop with your physical progress. As you begin to gain more control over your self-esteem, remember that your emotions can lift you up and give you improved self-esteem, too.

Continue to take the time to assess your emotional state on a regular basis because your response to any emotion you feel determines how you show up in the world. Working on your responses takes as much conscious thought and effort as making healthy food choices and exercising regularly. Every time you springboard from emotion, you build resiliency.

Use affirmations like these:

Anger: I'm upset right now with what's happened, but I resolve to find a solution like I know I can.

Despair: I screwed up this project. It's not the end because I'm good at *DASH* and *DASH*. What happened is a learning experience.

Frustration: I am going to see this project to the end, and I'll feel successful because I completed it.

The key lies in making a reasonable observation rather than crafting a pie-in-the-sky ideal like *"I'm going to be awesome"* and then affirming your positive qualities. Psychologist Guy Winch reminds those working on affirmations for self-esteem to practice these skills just as they would nutrition and exercise habits.

Courage Hacks: The Secret Habits of Confident People

Confident people use multiple techniques to boost their self-esteem. No one strategy works all the time. Some of the techniques, like diet and exercise are honed over time. Others can be implemented right away. Try the following quick tips to improve your self-esteem and produce confidence quickly.

Personal

Take small moments (in the elevator or during the time it takes to turn on your computer) to engage in visualizations, prayer, or meditation.

Prepare for tomorrow *today*. Select (and iron) your clothes the night before you wear them. Put your planner, purse, briefcase, kids' homework and permission slips, or anything else that you have to take with you in a single location so that you're not searching for the items in the morning. Make quiet time for yourself every day, even if that means spending three minutes in your closet or in your car reflecting on the day you've had or envisioning tomorrow.

Social

Learn names and faces by noticing what's unique about the person and creating a mental association to help you remember them. Remember birthdays and anniversaries by checking your social media pages daily or keep a master list on your calendar or computer. If you're sending snail mail cards, purchase them once a month. The sign and address them for delivery, writing the send date (7 days early) where the postage stamp will go.

Commit to others. People who live the longest are often those who have something to live for. Get involved with a group or donate your time; the more you give, the more you will get in return.

Professional

Schedule your day in advance. Write down the most important tasks first and block out time for them. The small ones will take care of themselves. Welcome the crisis du jour because it will come whether you are ready or not. Schedule only 80% of your day. Allow the remaining 20% of your time for dealing with interruptions and emergencies. On the rare days you have neither, use the time for yourself or to get ahead on something else.

Make a pro-level bug-out bag. Survivalists depend on bug-out bags filled with emergency medical supplies and food.

Make one for your self-esteem. Gather meaningful quotes, mementos that inspire courage, a journal and pencil, even a few granola bars and a bottle of water. When your self-esteem needs a lift, grab your bag, go to a favorite spot, and spend some time reflecting on the strategies you've been using.

Going Forward In Life

As you look to your future, welcome experiences and challenges. Be open to the possibility of change, including meeting people and taking on new opportunities. You'll feel a new purpose and meaning in life, and your self-esteem and confidence will soar.

Open your world with strategies like these:

Use social media to make connections beyond your microcosm. Be willing to initiate and accept friend requests in your social media accounts, keeping in mind that these acquaintances can expand your network.

Work with a friend, mentor, or coach. Although you may have hundreds or even thousands of social media "friends," the human connection and relationships built on trust are powerful insulators of self-esteem.

Keep a Courage Notebook. Writing down your accomplishments helps you identify and celebrate them. On the verso page (the right-hand side of the open notebook) record at least one daily act of courage. On the recto page (the right side page) explain how the action made you feel. Store the notebook in your pro-level bug out bag so you can reread it when you need reminding that you are confident and courageous.

Finally, dare to be vulnerable by not knowing everything. Being vulnerable opens up possibility, and when you welcome the unknown, you also increase your self–confidence.

Above all, ***stay true to yourself***. Having positive self-esteem isn't about being the loudest voice in the room; it's about having an *authentic* voice. Accept yourself for who you are and be confident in that role.

"I don't regret the things I've done. I regret the things I didn't do when I had the chance."
Unknown Author

Your opportunity is here. You have the chance now. Confidence comes from practice. Every day that you do one thing to boost your self-esteem, you're exercising your confidence muscle. Muscles get stronger through regular use, and so will your self-esteem.

You don't have to live your life like Leslie, Joe or Wendy. They've accepted the cards they've been dealt, and they are living from hour to hour and day. Their limiting beliefs and assumptions are holding them back and confining their self-esteem. That's *not* you. You are meant to be the best possible version of yourself. You have the tools you need.

You are confident. Bold. Courageous.
Thanks for reading. I wish you luck in your journey.

How To Overcome Anxiety & Worry Through Mindfulness.

Deal with worry, stress, panic, fear & negative thinking.

Michelle Galler

Copyright © Michelle Galler Publishing

All rights reserved.
No part of this publication may be reproduced, distributed, or transmitted in any form or by any means, including photocopying, recording, or other electronic or mechanical methods, without the prior written permission of the publisher, except in the case of brief quotations embodied in critical reviews and certain other non-commercial uses permitted by copyright law.

Beating Anxiety and Worry

"Yesterday is not ours to recover, but tomorrow is ours to win or lose."
Lyndon B. Johnson

Living life in a constant state of anxiety and worry is no fun at all. It curtails your enjoyment of even the simplest things as you fret about what might go wrong or how inadequate you feel. It doesn't take much to shift from being just about able to cope to being overwhelmed. By definition, the last straw that breaks the camel's back is a tiny, insignificant thing in itself, but a tiny thing too far when added to everything else weighing you down.
The good news is that there are strategies and approaches which can help. You can take back control. It won't happen overnight, but gradually you will find things are just that bit better. It's a journey towards rediscovering the joy in life, and an all-important first step on that journey is reading this book.

The 21st-century lifestyle is wonderful in many ways. We live longer than ever before, we have better education, healthcare, and housing than our predecessors. We can travel across the world in a matter of hours and be in touch with distant friends and family instantly through the magic of digital communications. There is a lot to be grateful for.

But our modern way of living is also incredibly stressful. Social media and the Internet can become an addiction, and the endless pressure to present your best self leading a dream life can lead to feelings of inadequacy and failure. We are bombarded 24/7 by information, far too much for us to consciously process. At work, the same digital devices that bring us entertainment and diversion make us constantly accessible, meaning we can never really switch off from the stream of *"urgent"* communications pinging, bleeping or flashing at us, demanding our attention.

An avalanche of media articles, TV shows, books, celebrity opinions, YouTube tutorials and guru blogs on every aspect of our personal lives from dating and relationships to child rearing and house interiors lead to us feeling like lesser beings if our homes aren't clutter-free and sparkling, our partners and children not perfect and loving and our bodies anything except lithe and youthful, clad in the latest designer must-haves. It can get utterly exhausting keeping up with the Millennials, no wonder we all want to crawl into a hole and hide sometimes!

Worry is an insidious and unhelpful emotion. It achieves nothing. Engaging in worry just makes you feel bad, which in turn makes you more likely to worry and less able to cope. It's a vicious circle that can be hard to escape. It takes a lot of determination to break the cycle of worry, but it is so worth breaking. Expending precious energy fretting about something that either may not happen or that you can do nothing about, really is a waste. Here's a little story to make the point.

Two friends, Kathy and Maria, invested their life savings in a company that looked like a good bet. For a while, things went well and then one day the company's shares nosedived. It looked like they would lose everything. They would find out at 4pm if they were bankrupt or not. Before everything happened, they had arranged to play a round of golf, and so they met in the golf course changing room.

Kathy was singing as she changed into her golf clothes. Meanwhile, Maria was on her phone, worried sick. She looked at her friend.

"How can you even think about playing golf today? We could be penniless in a few hours," she said.

"Well," Kathy replied. *"We can't do anything until four. Yes, we may lose everything, or we may not. But it's out of our hands Maria. If I could do something, I would. But since I can't, I'm not going to waste energy thinking about it. I'm going to go out and whack a few balls! Coming?"*

"No, I think I'll stay here. Someone might have some news before four, I need to stay put and, well, you know…"

"OK, see you later," Kathy said and off she went. Maria didn't notice. She was trying to get online to check the latest figures.

Kathy spent the next few hours breathing in fresh air, getting some exercise and enjoying her hobby. She whacked some balls pretty hard too and released some tension that way!
Maria spent the time pacing up and down, checking her phone every minute or so and calling friends to discuss the dire situation. By five to four she had a headache and felt truly sick and exhausted. She slumped on the bench and was still sitting there when her friend returned rosy-cheeked from her round of golf…
What happened at four o'clock? Well, that isn't the point, is it?

Making the choice to take some action is a positive and decisive step in the right direction. If you decide that enough is enough and that you want to re-experience the bright side of life, then you are already half-way there. Once you have made the decision, then things become just that bit easier, as if the very act itself has the power to effect change.
If you read it all the way through, then this book will be your guide to combatting overwhelm, worry and anxiety. The first part looks at the background and the theory because it helps to understand what is going on in your mind when you get into this state. The second part is a series of practical techniques you can use immediately to improve things.

This isn't a promise to make everything in the garden of your life rosy. *Nothing* is easy and perfect all the time. We *all* have to deal with the thorns as well as the roses. But having the right attitude and strategies in place makes it possible to appreciate and focus on the beauty of the flowers rather than the ugliness of the weeds. Rooting out worry and cutting back anxiety slowly and systematically helps create a light, bright space for good things to grow.

So, with no further ado, let us don our metaphorical gardening gloves, roll up our sleeves and begin!

PART 1: BEATING ANXIETY & STRESS

In order to change, you first need to understand what you are dealing with.
This section of the book will give you a background and a foundation to build on.

The Defining Terms

"Every problem has in it the seeds of its own solution. If you don't have any problems, you don't get any seeds."
Norman Vincent Peale

It always helps to know what you're dealing with, because then you can decide on the best strategy. This part of the book is going to look at the problems associated with anxiety and stress and their causes.

The chances are that you feel as if you can't cope. Things may have slowly built up to such an extent that you now spend your whole time in a state of chronic anxiety. You may feel like it wouldn't take much for you to lose it altogether and that you are just keeping hold of things by the most fragile of threads.

If you feel like this, then you will be suffering from at least one of the following problems:
Overwhelm
Worry
Anxiety
Fear
Panic
Stress

Let's look at them in turn. Not to wallow, that's not good, but to put them under the microscope and understand how they are all inter-connected.

Overwhelm
The fact that we use the verb *"overwhelm"* to describe being swamped by a huge mass, usually water, gives you a big clue to its meaning when applied to someone's psychological state. The Cambridge English dictionary defines overwhelm as *"to cause someone to feel sudden, strong emotion."*

The feeling of being overwhelmed can be a positive or a negative one. When you look at the starry sky above you on a clear night, it can be overwhelming, as can falling in love or being presented with an award. But the negative side of this emotional deluge is very unpleasant indeed. It is often used in a work context when the number of tasks you need to cram into one day threatens to swallow you up. Or you may feel helpless and powerless as you are bombarded from all sides by countless problems - *"the slings and arrows of outrageous fortune."* (Yes, even Shakespeare wrote about overwhelm!)

Feeling helpless is a common symptom of overwhelm, perhaps reawakening childhood memories of not being able to control your life. Very often we blame outside forces or circumstances rather than ourselves. You may say *"What next?"* as you open an unexpected tax bill, or *"why do these things always happen at the worst possible time?"* as the washing machine floods all over the cat.

Paralysis is a typical response to overwhelm. You may literally sit motionless, not knowing what to do next, or the paralysis may manifest as procrastination as you find yourself watching talking rabbit videos on YouTube instead of finishing your urgent report.

Another reaction to overwhelm is to become super-busy, as if you can somehow overcome the feeling of helplessness by sheer willpower and hard effort. In this situation, super-busy usually does not equal efficient or careful. You may make stupid mistakes if working with your mind, or become very clumsy if doing physical work.

Worry and Anxiety
There is an interesting article in **Psychology Today by Guy Winch: 10 Crucial Differences Between Worry and Anxiety.** In this, he describes how there are different psychological states, and we actually experience them differently. *"We tend to experience worry in our heads and anxiety in our bodies,"* he writes, adding later: *"worry is verbally focused while anxiety includes ... mental imagery."* Another interesting distinction is that *"worry often triggers problem-solving, but anxiety does not."* Winch's article goes on to explain that while worry can be short-term, controllable and often caused by realistic concerns, anxiety can be longer-term, cause serious emotional distress and can even *"jump from one focus to another."*

Fear and Panic
Fear is the feeling of being scared by a specific real or imagined danger. The focus is usually short term – the present and immediate future. If it spirals out of control fear can lead to panic. An example of a real fear would be getting hit by a train if your car breaks down on a level crossing. An example of an imagined fear would be that there is someone hiding under your bed as you lie there in the dark. Whether real or imagined, with fear, you want to escape from the situation, or avoid it in the first place.

Stress
"Don't stress me out!"
"I'm so stressed!"
"This is really causing me stress!"

We use the term *"stress"* a lot these days, probably without really understanding what it means.

Back in the days when we lived in caves, life was genuinely dangerous. There were myriad of scary things, from wild animals to hostile neighbors, ready to snuff us out in a heartbeat. When we detected a threat, our bodies flooded us with chemicals to enable us to fight or run. The three major stress hormones adrenaline, cortisol, and norepinephrine, were released, moving blood from non-crucial areas like the skin to crucial ones like the muscles, increasing arousal, heart rate, breathing rate and responses. All good news in a life-threatening situation. And once the danger was over the chemicals would dissipate and you could return to cooking mammoth meatballs or doing something creative with flint.

The world has moved on from the dinosaur age to the digital and now our *"threats"* are things like huge credit card bills or an impossible boss; not lions looking for lunch. But, sadly, in those thousands of intervening years, we poor humans have not changed that much. Our brains still flood us with stress hormones whenever a threat appears, even if it is not a genuinely life-threatening one. Because we can't work off the stress chemicals by running or fighting, they slosh around our bodies with nowhere to go. Ironically, what nature designed to save us is now hurting us. Adrenaline, cortisol, and norepinephrine cause all manner of symptoms, particularly if you are constantly in situations which *"stress you out"*.

Chronic stress is no good for you at all. Some of the main symptoms are:

- insomnia
- headaches
- digestive problems *(from nausea and diarrhea to constipation and bloating)*
- loss of appetite or overeating
- drinking alcohol more
- smoking more
- substance abuse
- low energy
- low sex drive
- weak immune system
- skin problems
- inability to concentrate
- inability to make decisions
- inability to finish things
- lack of interest in anything outside work
- irritability
- anger or suppressed anger

It is important to mention that not *all* stress is bad. Apart from helping in genuinely dangerous situations, some acute stress is beneficial and can help motivate you to achieve more, improve your performance and overcome obstacles. This good stress is called eustress, and it can feel exciting. A typical characteristic of eustress is that you have a lot of control over the outcome and feel you can cope. Afterwards, you may feel on a high, tingling with the thrill of success.

The Causes of Stress
There are many specific situations which you can immediately identify as understandable causes of negative stress. These include:
- death of a spouse or loved one
- divorce
- separation
- money problems
- conflict or problems with children, family or friends
- legal problems
- illness or injury (yourself or loved ones)
- unemployment or job insecurity
- being a victim of crime or abuse

Some causes of **positive** stress include:
- getting married
- changing jobs
- moving house
- having a baby
- retiring
- getting promoted
- winning or inheriting money

However, there are many other contributors to stress which you may not be aware of, but which chip away at you insidiously. Many of these are products of our 21st-century lifestyle and can include:
- information overload from email, internet, social media and other digital sources
- multi-tasking

- 24/7 news which is inevitably tragic or sensational and creates a feeling that the world is a dangerous and volatile place
- commuting and travel
- over scheduling
- perfectionism or unrealistic expectations *(perhaps created by celebrity culture, social media or mass media)*
- fears and phobias

Real Life Case Study: Serena

Serena Harvey is 39 years old and lives in a small seaside town in the south of the UK. She has been married for two years and has just had a baby, Amelia. She used to work in advertising and her husband Mike is a woodcarver and artist. They live in a small two-bedroomed house a few miles from the town center, which has a tiny garden and is within walking distance of the shops and a park. She was always close to her parents, but her mother died three years ago, and her father isn't coping very well. Serena has been feeling increasingly stressed and anxious since Amelia was born. This is what she says:

"In two years, I have changed from being a career girl, owning my own flat and bringing home quite good money to being a wife and a mother. It has been a real shock to the system.

Don't get me wrong, I love Mike and Amelia to bits. I got married and had a baby relatively late so it's not like I haven't had time to enjoy myself and travel and feel free. Oh my God, just listen to me! Talking about feeling free as if I'm in prison. I know I should be counting my blessings. I have a roof over my head, a guy who loves me, a gorgeous little girl... I don't know what's the matter with me really. I just feel so stressed all the time, like I'm going to explode. I've seen the doctor and I know it's not post-natal depression or anything like that. My friend Natalie had post-natal depression and it's not something you mess around with. No, this is just feeling generally, oh I don't know, just anxious, on edge. Hard to know how to describe it really. I seem to have so many things to do every day, I don't know where the time goes. Sometimes I just feel completely overwhelmed."

From what we already know about major life events, it's not surprising that Serena is feeling stressed. She has had a baby, and her sleeping patterns and lifestyle have changed. You can imagine that Serena is tired and although it is three years since her mum died, she must be missing her, particularly as a grandmother to her little girl. Let's find out a bit more about what's going on:

"Mike is brilliant, he does as much as he can to help me, but he's just got a new commission for a series of sculptures and needs to focus on that. I envy him the fact he's working. I do miss my job. I mean it was crazy a lot of the time, but I enjoyed the drama and the ridiculous deadlines if I'm honest. And the sense of teamwork. I don't really see many people at the moment and a lot of my old friends are from work and our schedules are very different now."

"Our financial situation is pretty precarious as he's freelance. We've had to borrow on the credit cards to get stuff for the house and Amelia. I find that hard, I used to

earn good money. I hate scrimping and watching every penny! We don't owe a lot, not like my friend Casey who owes more than 20 grand. But I hate owing money and what with that and the mortgage we don't have a lot of spare cash. My Mum left me a little bit, a few thousand, but that's all long gone."

Serena has financial worries to add to the mix. Not serious ones, her husband has a new commission and they bring in enough to pay the mortgage, but they can't spend without thinking.

In addition to the practical issues that are bound to be stressful for anyone – death of a parent, a new baby, some financial pressures – there are those individual stressors that are so subjective and powerful. Serena is used to being independent, relatively carefree and well-off, working in a fast paced and quite exciting environment. Now her husband is the breadwinner and she spends most of her day at home. Her language at the start, the talk of freedom and prisons, is quite revealing.

We will come back to Serena throughout the book as she is going to try some of the ideas and techniques and give her feedback. One important thing to emphasize, whatever situation you are in, is that you should not feel guilty or think there is anything wrong with you because you have these feelings. It means that you are human.

Chapter 1 Takeaways

In this chapter we have looked at:
- The main components of stress and anxiety

- How stress manifests itself and a list of common symptoms
- The main causes of stress, worry and overwhelm
- The Holmes-Rahe stress test
- A case study involving Serena, a stressed new mother and former career girl who is feeling guilty for missing her freedom and overwhelmed by her current life

Now that we have analyzed the components of stress, anxiety and worry we will tackle an area that is a constant cause of emotional overwhelm for a lot of us - relationships. They can be the cause of such joy, but also the cause of many of our problems. Let's try and understand why.

Chapter 2 - The Stress of Relationships

"Nobody can hurt me without my permission."
Mahatma Gandhi

There are many different kinds of relationship, and you probably bring different aspects of your personality and character to each one. How you behave with your work colleagues may be completely different to how you are with your cousins or your partner or even your dog! What won't change, however, are your fundamental values and your way of being.

Motivational speaker Jim Rohn says you are the average of the five people you spend the most time with. I would say that should be six people because the person you spend all the time with is…you.

The Most Important Relationship In Your Life

The most important relationship of all is the one you have with yourself. Like it or not, you are going to be in it for the long term! By definition, relationships involve more than one person, so how can you have a relationship with yourself? Well, you are made of many parts, a community of inter-connected members. You have a relationship with your body and a relationship with your mind.

It's interesting to consider who the *"you"* is in that last sentence. When you think to yourself: *"I feel stressed,"* who is the one noticing that you feel stressed? It would appear that there is an *"observer"* part of you that notices and comments on these things. In other words, because you can think about your thinking, it means you are not your thoughts and emotions; you are separate from them. This can be very liberating because you realize that there is an authentic *"you"* that can operate independently from all the chaos and crap surrounding you.

To develop a healthy and nourishing relationship with yourself, first of all, you need to become an observer of yourself, to notice what triggers certain behavior, what pushes your buttons. That doesn't mean you have to try and correct that behavior, simply to notice it. The more you do this, the more powerful your observer mind will become, and the weaker your unhelpful responses will become. If you practice observing what is going on in your mind on a regular basis, you will begin to develop new neural pathways which will strengthen over time.

Understanding the observer mind can be one of the most powerful things you can do to develop a good relationship with yourself. Other things to do are:

Practice self-care.
This concerns your physical body. Make sure you nourish yourself by eating well, drinking enough water, getting enough sleep and exercise.

Have fun and reward yourself.
Do things that make you feel good, smile or laugh out loud. If you want to play on the swings in the park – do it! Watch a funny movie or your favorite stand-up comedian on YouTube. Give yourself treats every day, like half an hour reading a great novel or eating a delicious bar of chocolate. You deserve it!

Learn to meditate.
It need only take a few minutes every day but can have an incredible impact on all aspects of your life.

Take time to dream.
What would you like to do? How would you like your future to look? Write or draw (or paste pictures of) your dream life. Then spend a few minutes each day just imagining...

Create.
It doesn't matter if it's baking a cake, painting a picture, carving a piece of wood, writing a poem or knitting. Try to make sure that by the end of every day, you have created something that didn't exist in the morning.

Be compassionate.
Be as kind and caring to yourself as you would to other people. If you have had a terrible day, then treat yourself gently, as you would with a good friend who is feeling down. Don't beat yourself up for not feeling lively, energetic and positive. You are a human being, experiencing all the highs and lows that entails.

Research ways to help with problems.
If you are suffering from anxiety and stress, then spend some time researching how best to deal with it. Reading this book is a good start!

Relationships With Partners

Your relationship with your partner can affect you profoundly, particularly if you spend a lot of time together.

Think about yourself and your partner like two circles. When you decide to create a long-term relationship, the circles will overlap because of the experiences and beliefs you share. What you want to ensure is that one circle does not eclipse the other, that your whole life is subsumed into that of your partner. There should always be a separate part of the circles which is your own private space. As the circles grow and expand, so should the shared part. But it should always be in proportion.

Change is an inevitable and necessary part of any exclusive relationship. Its management is critical to the success of that relationship. Maintain an interest in your partner, what they think, how they behave, what they enjoy, how they look. Don't take them for granted.

As someone grows and matures, they will naturally change. The person may also make an active effort to change some aspect of their life, for example quitting smoking or losing weight. But don't ever force anyone to change or think that you can wait it out, and once you have been together long enough you can impose your ideas and will on your partner. It is the basis of the old (and sexist) joke: *What three words about weddings sum up a bride's attitude towards her future husband? Aisle, altar, hymn!* The only person you can change in any relationship is yourself.

Anxiety can ruin an intimate relationship, making you doubt everything. Continually fretting about if your partner is faithful or really does love you will mean that you may constantly be seeking reassurance. Everyone needs some reassurance of course, but too much can turn into neediness, which is not an attractive trait.

Alternatively, anxiety may make you withdraw and not allow yourself to show any vulnerability. You may even provoke situations in order to *"prove"* to yourself that you were right all along and the relationship was doomed. You may even nip fledgling relationships in the bud before they have a chance to develop because you are worried about getting hurt if you give your heart away. It becomes a self-fulfilling prophecy.

A healthy relationship means both partners trust each other but can also be vulnerable with each other. You have to accept that you deserve to be loved and to be treated well. Your partner loves you, your quirky ways and your uniqueness. You don't have to be perfect, you just have to be yourself; that is good enough. And if by chance it isn't good enough, and you can see that they are trying to change you, then they don't deserve you.

It's so nice to be relaxed with your partner, even when you're in old clothes and your hair's a mess. Who wouldn't want to feel that comfortable with their special someone? But that doesn't mean you should stop making an effort. So, dress up sometimes like you did on the first date. Keep the spark alive! I know a couple who have been married for 16 years and they always dress up for dinner, even at home. They say it's a daily reminder not to take their relationship for granted. You don't have to go to that extreme, but a spontaneous gift, a loving touch or asking about their day *(and listening with attention to the answer)* go a long way to keeping an intimate relationship fresh. It also keeps anxiety at bay, because your attention is on making your partner feel loved and appreciated, not on how worried you feel.

Another thing you can do if you are feeling worried in your relationship is to practice the observer tactic I mentioned earlier. Watch yourself worry! Accept that everyone worries and that you are not a bad person for doing that. Then try something. Act as if you haven't got any worries at all. As if everything in your relationship is perfect. Even if you do it for only a limited time, like an hour, it is very powerful.

No relationship is perfect and if you're anxious, you won't want to address problems in case it causes everything to end. But sometimes you need to talk about things that are bothering you or they could, over time, develop into a serious issue. Little things are more damaging than big things because the big problems are often things that can be tackled together.
You need to look at how you handle issues that bother you. Always use the first person and say how something makes you feel, rather than dictating what the other person should or should not be doing. So, for instance, you say *"I feel quite upset when you don't answer my texts straight away,"* rather than *"you never answer my texts straight away. What's the matter with you? I always reply to you immediately!"*

Some issues can't be fixed. If the anxiety you are feeling is caused by a toxic or co-dependent relationship, if your partner abuses you mentally or physically or does anything other than support you and love you, then you need to acknowledge the damage it is doing to you and move on, even though it might be hard to accept.

Your Relationship With Your Kids

"We never know the love of a parent till we become parents ourselves."
Henry Ward Beecher

There is no bond on earth like that of parent and child and because of its unconditional nature, there is also no bond likely to cause you more anxiety, worry and pain. So how can you build a healthy relationship with your child?

One of the most important things you can do is to spend time with your kids. Be present. Actively listen to them and be there for them as a loving and stable anchor. That means not multi-tasking or interrupting their bedtime story or chat time to take a call from work. It also means regularly making sure you have free time for them, because quantity does matter, despite what they say about "quality time" being more important. Your kids need to know they are a priority in your life.

Trust is a crucial issue in a parent and child relationship, from when they are tiny to when they tower over you. Be a good example. Don't break promises or confidences. Trust that they are doing the best they can and believe them if they tell you something. That doesn't mean being gullible and letting them lie to you, but thinking the best of them and allowing them to make their own mistakes sometimes.

Children respond well to encouragement and praise, yet it is all too easy to yell and criticize. Be supportive and positive while still being realistic. Don't lead kids to believe they are always right or that they will never fail. Things go wrong, that's part of life. Making mistakes and not always getting what you have set out to achieve are good life lessons, because it's not what happens to you that's important but how you deal with it. Being realistic doesn't mean being negative. I have a friend, Jeanie, whose mother believes in always being *"realistic."* (Yes, the parent–child bond doesn't disappear just because you are an adult.) She regularly pours cold water on Jeanie's plans and ideas, often pointing out so many potential flaws that Jeanie gives up before she's begun.

If your relationship with your child is causing you anxiety, then take a step back and examine things objectively. When children are growing up they are trying to make sense of the world, testing boundaries and learning to understand their own emotions. They are childish! They may lie, or get angry and lash out at you, but it isn't usually personal. They don't really hate you and wish you were dead! Over-reaction is a part of being a child, particularly a moody, hormonal teen. Getting riled and shouting at them is not going to help matters. Keep as calm as you can, don't raise your voice, and remember *"this too shall pass."* You are the adult here; you are the one that should set an example of how to behave, rather than get drawn into a slanging match.

Often parents project their own hopes and dreams onto their kids, getting worried and frustrated when things don't work out or when they feel their child isn't putting in enough effort. Be careful you are not living your life through your child, for example, encouraging them to do something they are not interested in or good at because secretly you always wanted to do it but never could.

A very good piece of advice is to put yourself in your children's shoes, perhaps even trying to think back to when you were their age and how you felt. A five-year-old has very different concerns from a fifteen-year-old, so don't dismiss their feelings and tell them it doesn't matter. Maybe it does to them. That doesn't mean giving in and letting them have everything they want; it means acknowledging what they have said and then setting fair boundaries.

Apparently, having dinner together as a family is extremely beneficial, even if just one parent is present. Take time to eat with your kids, ideally at the table, rather than with food on your laps and the TV on.

It isn't rocket science to point out that kids and adults these days are absolutely glued to their cell phones or other devices. Social media is a big cause of anxiety too, so set a good example yourself. Beware of the temptation to use technology as a babysitter, particularly if your children are young. Introduce them to nature, to books and animals. Show them there is life away from the screen!

Children learn by example, so if you are feeling worried and anxious in your own life and show it, they will pick up on this and perhaps even copy it. Learning to manage your own fears and feelings is an excellent model for your kids. You can even get them to identify how they are feeling and teach them techniques to cope. For example, counting to ten before saying anything if they feel angry or taking a few deep breaths if they feel scared.

The Relationship With Family and Friends

"You can't choose your family, but thank goodness you can choose your friends," so the old saying goes. Your family has the power to bring great joy but also cause you to have a lot of self-doubt and anguish. Let's face it, no-one can push your buttons as effectively as someone who has known you since you were a little kid!

It is all too easy to get into serious fights with your siblings and parents or parents-in-law. In my own family, there are several past incidences of family members not speaking for months or even years. Life is too short for this. Every family problem affects your energy and tugs at your subconscious and it is worth reaching out and healing a rift. Unless you are actually suffering abuse and damage, physical or psychological, then mend fences, say sorry, even if something wasn't your fault, and build a relationship with them again. I remember my friend John telling me that his elderly mother and her brother hadn't spoken for years. Then his mother got seriously ill. *"I called up my uncle,"* he said. *"And I told him my mom was very ill. I asked if the worst happened, would he would come to my mother's funeral. He was very shocked and replied of course he would. I told him that if he would do that, then wouldn't it be better to visit while she was still alive and they could enjoy time together. He came over the following week."*

Family members and those grafted onto us by marriage or partnerships can be demanding, and you may feel the need to be always in control and perfect which will cause a lot of stress and anxiety. I am giving you express permission to leave the beautiful housework skills, magical cleaning ability and immaculate child-rearing to the gods and goddesses of this world. You are good enough. If the house isn't 100 percent tidy when the in-laws come round, so be it. No one is shooting at you. It is not a life or death situation. There will always be clean freaks who will run a metaphorical white-gloved finger over the tops of your doors to check for dust. Well, good for them. You may prefer to spend the polishing time playing with the kids or writing a poem or even just doing nothing. That is your choice. It is your life. You can't please everyone.

Friends are a gift and research has proved that the better your social life and the wider your circle of friends, the healthier and happier you are. Even those of us who adore being alone and would rather stay in with a good book than go to a party can enjoy spending time with people who make us feel loved and uplifted.
 It takes two to tango, and the same goes for friendship. It is a give and take process and even if you are feeling depressed and stressed, don't forget to call a friend on their birthday, send a note thanking someone who has been kind, or just remind someone that their friendship means a lot. It is also OK to ask for help if you are feeling down. This is something you might find hard to do if you are the one who usually cheers people up or is known for being the life and soul of the party. I know this from personal experience. You feel like your role is to be the comforter and not the one needing comforting. But you are entitled to ask for support if you need it and your friends may be delighted to switch roles for a change, even slightly relieved that you are not perfect and positive the whole time!

There is one caveat with friendships and that is to beware of the toxic kind. You know exactly what I mean. The person who makes you feel depressed every time you are with them. Who is negative and judgmental and critical. Who seems to think your role is to be their sounding board as they rant on about all the things that make them angry or depressed or upset or, or, or … There is only one thing to do with people like this and that is limit your contact with them! It can be hard to just cut a relationship off, so just make sure you are busy or make an excuse if they demand your time. No-one needs energy vampires.

Chapter 2 Take-Aways

All the types of relationship we have looked at have the possibility of causing you tremendous worry and stress or great happiness and fulfillment. Which one it ends up being is in your hands, because you are the one in charge of your emotions and how you respond. In this chapter you have learned:

- The most significant and long-lasting relationship is the one you have with yourself. So be true to yourself. Don't fake anything.

- You need to limit or end toxic or co-dependent relationships.

- In relationships, particularly intimate ones, you must not be afraid of being yourself.

- Neediness can spoil things. You are worth loving.

- In all relationships, be assertive and explain what you need.

- That children need attention, time and encouragement. Be a good example.

- How relationships are a two-way process.

- The power of laughter and doing things that bring you joy.

- How anything worthwhile takes work and time.

In the next chapter we'll look at how you can get to know yourself better and make plans to change the way you react to worry and stress. Let's take a deep breath and dive in!

Chapter 3 - Creating Your Future

"They always say time changes things, but you actually have to change them yourself."
Andy Warhol

Changing isn't as difficult as you think. The hardest thing is actually making the decision to change. We can produce endless excuses, we can procrastinate like champions, we can convince ourselves that *"it's better the devil you know,"* in order to avoid taking that all-important step!

You purchased this book because you are not happy with how your life is at the moment. You have recognized that you are allowing anxiety and worry to play too big a role in your life. That, in itself, is significant. You don't have to criticize yourself or beat yourself up about it. Wanting things to be better than they are now is a very positive acknowledgment. No-one is perfect, we all have flaws and problems to deal with. Stage one is to own up to the issue and you have done that.

The next stage is to admit that things can't go on as they are. We all deserve to live the most fulfilled life possible and make the most of all the amazing opportunities that surround us. We need to have enough inner strength to be able to deal with the lows as well as the highs, because life isn't always all sunshine and rainbows. If you are governed by fear and worry, then all your energy will go towards feeding those negative emotions. You will be constantly tossed around on a gray sea of negativity. It has to stop. In its place, you need equilibrium and a calm center.

The good news is that you have all the tools at your disposal to help you change. There are many things you can do to improve your situation. They don't cost any money and they aren't that hard to follow. All you need do is resolve to try them, to give them a chance to work. That's fair enough, isn't it? It's amazing how empowered you will feel once you start practicing a few of the techniques that will be outlined in this book.
Your brain will begin to make changes very fast as it learns new modes of operating. You will build up new neural networks. Your subconscious will get the message that you are someone who responds to situations in a positive and proactive way and this will get reinforced the more you do it.

Aristotle famously said, *"We are what we repeatedly do."* Things we repeatedly do are, of course, habits. In some ways, our whole lives are governed by habits, some we are conscious of, some not. Habits which benefit us are positive and helpful, however we usually have a load of habits that are not making our lives better or more meaningful, quite the reverse. American author and philosopher Henry James wrote in his essay Habit in 1887: *"The great thing, then, in all education, is to make our nervous system our ally instead of our enemy. It is to fund and capitalize our acquisitions, and live at ease upon the interest of the fund. For this we must make automatic and habitual, as early as possible, as many useful actions as we can, and guard against the growing into ways that are likely to be disadvantageous to us, as we should guard against the plague."*

An important thing to do is to examine your habits, keep those that are beneficial, ditch those that are not and replace them with new, good habits.

Research shows that it takes between 21 days and 66 days to develop a new habit to the stage where it becomes automatic. The length of time depends on how complex or demanding the new habit is. If, for example, you want to drink an extra glass of water every day, you could probably make that an automatic part of your routine in three weeks, because it isn't that challenging a task. If you want to regularly monitor your thoughts and stop yourself in the act of negative self-talk, it will take longer than that. But as with anything, persistence pays off. Setting a time frame is a good idea. If you are the type of person who likes lists, plans and written targets then you will feel very comforted and motivated by having a strategy in place, even if you only take baby steps.

Talking of baby steps, there is a book called **Mini Habits** by *Stephen Guise*, based on the idea that taking tiny actions consistently every day can achieve great results. The author himself achieved peak physical fitness in two years by starting with just one push-up a day. Sometimes the thought of change can be so overwhelming and such a mountain to climb that you end up doing nothing. Getting into the habit of doing one *"small silly thing"* regularly every day can have a huge impact. It's like the old saying, *"How do you eat an elephant? One bite at a time."*

Dealing With Your Issues

The Greek philosopher Socrates once said that *"the unexamined life is not worth living."* What did he mean by that? After all, the language is quite extreme! I think he was pointing out that as human beings we need to take time to reflect on our own lives, identify our personal values, habits, strengths and weaknesses. Taking some time to think constructively about your life and identify the areas needing improvement is a very useful exercise. Yet surprisingly few people do it.

What are the main things you want to change? As this book is about removing anxiety and worry from your life, then we will focus on those areas, rather than looking at your whole life. It's all too easy to get sucked down rabbit holes and get distracted from the main task. However, you can apply these techniques to all aspects of your life, once you have dealt with anxiety.

It is quite normal to worry about everyday issues; work, money, health, your family and so on. But if those worries become excessive and stop you functioning normally, then it is time to tackle them. When you find yourself anxious about every single thing, when you imagine murder, natural disaster or fatal accident if your partner is late or your child doesn't call, rather than the more likely scenario of forgetfulness or a switched-off cell phone, then maybe you need to do something about it.

It's a good idea to buy a notebook **(yes, the paper kind that you use with a pen!)** and use it to chart your issues and progress. Let's begin by looking at a list of things that might trigger your anxiety. Think about each one and over the next few days note down any thoughts and feelings you have and what you have observed.

Note down the time of day, the time of month, the time of year. There's lots of food for thought here. For example: Is there a particular time of day when you feel jittery? Could it be linked to certain drinks, food or being hungry? Or to darkness or light? The syndrome Seasonal Affective Disorder *(SAD)* is a well-known one, linking depression and dark moods to short winter days. Does a full moon have any effect on you? If you are of child-bearing age, how does your monthly period affect your mood?

Sleep: Are you getting enough? Do you dream or have nightmares? Maybe an anxiety dream triggers a waking mood of worry? Can you link different moods with your sleep patterns? Is your bedroom a calm haven and your bed a welcoming and cozy place? You may not take Feng Shui seriously, but they have a point regarding not having electronic devices in the bedroom, having a tidy space, not sleeping under beams and not having loads of stored items under your bed.

Health: You may not know it, but some physical health conditions produce anxiety as one of the symptoms, for example, an over-active thyroid, heart disease or high blood pressure. If you have any worries about your health, **have a check-up**. Do any foods, drinks or medicines trigger feelings of anxiety? Personally, Italian espresso coffee makes my nerves jangle and my heart race as well as making me feel extremely anxious, so I rarely drink it.

People and Their Habits: Are there people in your life who make you feel anxious or worried after an encounter with them? I have a friend who is very kind-hearted and generous, but has such a negative world view and is so critical of everyone and everything that I feel depressed every time we meet up! Do any family members trigger feelings of anxiety because of your past experience with them? Perhaps when you were a child, your grandmother was very superstitious and if she saw one sole magpie, would tell you terrible things would happen. These things go deeper than you imagine, and your unexplained and sudden feeling of gloom yesterday could be linked to a single black and white bird you didn't even think you had noticed consciously! The same goes for beliefs about money, work and family. If your parents were very concerned whenever a bill arrived then you could be producing the same response whenever a bill for you arrives, even if it is expected and you have enough money to pay it.

Your Environment: Is your living space clean and tidy? Spending a lot of time in an untidy, cramped or dirty environment can have a significant negative effect on you. If the corner of your living room is piled with bills and other unfiled paperwork, or you have stacks of laundry waiting to be ironed, boxes to unpack and so on, it can easily make you anxious and depressed. Every time you see this mess it will have an impact, even if you are not conscious of it. Do you have access to outside or to nature? Greenery, even pot plants, is a mood booster as well as helping you concentrate. Fresh air and sunshine not only boost Vitamin D but also make you feel better. Is your environment full of "sound and fury" or quiet and relaxing? Noise pollution can be as damaging as the physical kind. What can you see around you and how does it make you feel? Certain colors are more calming than others. Possessions and artwork can affect you because of the actual subject matter or the person you associate it with. If your bitchy mother-in-law gave you a painting then you will probably think of her every time you look at it, even if it is beautiful in itself!

Your Habits: As mentioned before, we are shaped by our habits, both good and bad. Do you do things mindlessly which may be having a negative impact? Maybe you always switch on the news at 7 o'clock because – well, you just do – and so your day starts with a depressing flood of nasty, anxiety-producing stories which don't personally affect you, but are presented as if they do. Do you add additional and unnecessary steps into a simple process, causing unneeded complication? It was only when I explained to my pet sitter that my dogs had a cup each of dogfood in the mornings, then a certain type of chew, then two small splashes of milk (not one, not three, but two) but that in the evening they had a cup of dogfood, a different chew and just one splash of milk otherwise they got upset, that I realized perhaps I was making a rod for my own back!

Major Life Events: Remember the stress test we did before? If you have had any of those things happen to you over the last 12 months then you are going to feel some degree of anxiety and stress on a daily basis. Inevitably, certain things, for example anniversaries, places or even music, will trigger feelings related to the event. It's quite normal, all you need do is note down when it happens in your notebook.

Sorting Through Your Anxiety Triggers

Once you have made notes over a few days, you can start to look at your personal stress and anxiety triggers and see if you notice any patterns. What you discover may surprise you. Just by doing this you have already taken an enormous step in reducing the stress in your life, because being aware of the problem is half the battle.

The next thing is to select one area to work on. Don't try to tackle it all at once even if you feel motivated to do so, because inevitably you will lose impetus and feel overwhelmed. Remember the elephant – one bite at a time!

This book will help, you can read it through first and then select the techniques you feel best suit the area you are working on. The exercises have been designed to be used in any sequence, so just pick something you feel drawn to. Not everything will be appropriate or suit your learning style. That's why it's important to have some idea about the kind of activities you enjoy doing and what kind of learner you are. Some people are highly visual, so enjoy any activities which involve images, drawing or creating mind pictures. Others work best with words and sounds, so will feel more drawn to exercises involving writing or music. Some of you are more kinesthetic, preferring to move around and try things out. *(You're the kind who will be playing around with the pieces of the wardrobe to see how they might fit together rather than reading the instruction manual!)* The point is, know yourself and your learning style and then use techniques to match. This includes your preferred time of day to practice. Be kind to yourself. Give yourself the best possible chance of success.

Talking of success, it's important to visualize a positive outcome after having eliminated one area of stress from your life. How would things change if worry about this problem was no longer an issue for you? What could you do? How would you feel? Imagine yourself happy and relaxed, ready to take the next step. If it helps you, then hand over your doubts and questions to a higher power – God, the Universe, it doesn't matter what you call this source of energy and love, just believe that your efforts are being guided and that you are not in this alone. It is achievable. You can do it.

Real Life Case Study: Remember Serena from Chapter 1? She's a 39-year-old former career girl and new mother who is feeling constantly stressed, but also feels guilty about feeling that way because she has a lovely little girl, a husband who adores her and a roof over her head. Serena decided to keep a small notebook handy and note down her stress and worry triggers and anything else she was feeling.

Time of day, time of month, time of year. As she did this in November, Serena noted that the dark mornings and evenings made her feel depressed and edgy. She remembered this was always the case and not just because of the new baby and the house move. Maybe she had Seasonal Affective Disorder? She circled "SAD" in her notebook as something to research later.

Sleep: This section made Serena laugh. What new mother gets enough sleep? She had always felt moody if she didn't get at least six hours, even when she was *"young, free and single"* so it wasn't surprising that night after night of interrupted sleep would affect her. She reasoned that it wouldn't last forever, in fact she had already noticed that Amelia was sleeping for a little longer each night.

Health: Serena had complete medical exams throughout her pregnancy and so knew that she was in general good health and had no underlying medical issues. She knew that pasta and wheat products made her lethargic and bloated and that dark chocolate could keep her awake, but in general she didn't really associate her anxiety with food or health.

People and Their Habits: Serena's father always used to say she had *"champagne tastes and a beer income"* and her mother, who had died so very recently, got incredibly anxious whenever bills arrived, particularly if she thought she had forgotten to pay them. Towards the end, she used to say she was terrified of going to prison is she was late paying a bill. This made Serena think. When she was working in advertising, she spent freely, without thinking. She made good money and basically had no-one to spend it on but herself. She always paid her bills on time and, quite unusually she thought, she only had one credit card, which she always paid in full every month. During the few days she was writing in her notebook several envelopes arrived, which her husband left unopened with the comment *"know what those are, don't need to see them!"* Serena noticed how upset and edgy this made her feel. She always opened the bills and faced the worst, it really annoyed her that Mike had a more relaxed attitude to money. She hated the fact they were living on one salary and had to struggle for money. Detested the fact they had bought stuff for Amelia and the new house with credit cards. She realized that she was behaving as anxiously as her mother used to, even worrying about losing their home or going to court because they couldn't pay their debts. *"Hmm,"* she said to herself as she underlined 'money' over and over again in her notebook. This was causing her a lot more stress than she had realized.

Your Environment: Serena's house was small, but she thought it was as tidy as it could be, considering the baby and all the things both she and Mike had brought with them from their previous single lives. It also had a little garden and lots of plants, as she and Mike loved being outside and nature. There was a lovely park nearby that she often went to with Amelia. She thought she probably got a good dose of fresh air and Vitamin D every day, so a big tick for that part! She looked around the room. Actually, there was quite a lot of stuff, including some ornaments and small items of furniture from her dear Mom's house which she wanted to have around to remind her of her childhood. She sat chewing her pen. Was she also hoping to hang onto her Mom's memory by keeping her stuff? She looked at one wall of the living room, which was almost a carbon copy of a wall in her Mom's place. She thought about how kind Mike had been when she started putting up Mom's clock and shelves and pictures. The house was really too small. It did make her feel kind of anxious when she saw all that stuff.

Your Habits: Serena thought long and hard about this part. She knew she wasn't suffering from OCD or any other type of compulsive disorder. Despite Mom's keepsakes, she wasn't a hoarder and she didn't need to do things a certain number of times or wash her hands a lot. She wasn't afraid of outdoors and although she enjoyed having her meals at set times – breakfast at 7, coffee at 11, lunch at 1, afternoon tea at 4 and dinner at 7 – she didn't think that was unusual. Was it? She remembered how she felt if this meal routine was disrupted. Very anxious. Hmmm. Amelia had certainly thrown her meals schedule out the window. Why was she so attached to this eating routine anyway? She circled this in her notebook, as something to do more thinking and research about as she felt it was one of her triggers.

Major Life Events: Serena made quick notes about the obvious major things that had happened to her within two years: a wedding, a death, leaving her job, a birth, a house move. *"It's surprising I can even get through the day in one piece with all that lot going on!"* she smiled to herself. After reading through her notes, Serena decided she was going to focus on reducing her anxiety over money as that was something that she was clearly getting very affected by. She reasoned that she couldn't really do anything about the life events, and that the other things could be tackled one by one. As a very visual person who also loved words and who was at her best in the early morning, she decided to start with exercises that matched her preferred learning style and to try them when she awoke at 6. We'll see how she gets on as we go through the book.

Chapter 3 Takeaways

In this chapter we have looked at:

- How taking the decision to change because things cannot go on as they are is an important step.

- The importance and power of habits and how long it takes to establish a new habit.

- Examining your life and identifying your stress and worry triggers

- How Serena tackled the stress triggers exercise and what she discovered about the sources of her own worries.

Now that you have looked at your own stress triggers and identified an area that you want to work on, you are ready for Part Two of the book; **Strategies for Success**. There you'll begin putting some of the ideas into practice. Ready?

PART 2: STRATEGIES FOR SUCCESS

This part of the book uses the knowledge from Part One as a foundation for different techniques to tackle worry and anxiety.

Chapter 4 - Creating Space and Making Changes

"Most of us are inclined to keep too many old and useless things in our houses and in our minds as well..."
Emily Tolman

It's hard to overestimate the importance of space, both inside and outside of us. We need a clear and clean environment if we are to thrive. Fill that inner or outer space with clutter, with *"stuff",* and we will soon find it hard to move and hard to breathe.

Very often someone's physical space will reflect their mental one. In a kind of vicious circle, your worry or anxiety will feed off that pile of unpaid bills or unopened mail in the corner of your living room. Stress will build as you subconsciously note all the things in your home that need to be repaired or thrown away. You may have a junk drawer, or a junk room, where you toss all the things you don't know how to deal with. Overwhelmed by the enormity of the task of clearing everything, you find it hard even to tidy one cupboard, which just makes you feel more anxious and annoyed with yourself.

Despite all the 21st-century services devoted to organizing and clutter clearing and the myriad gurus who want to save us from ourselves, clutter isn't a new problem. The Emily Tolman quote which opens this chapter is from a housekeeping book written in 1907. But the need to hold on to things whether we need them or not certainly dates back far earlier than that. Our prehistoric ancestors probably found it just as hard to part with their stuff. There's probably a huge junk room under Stonehenge filled with broken axes, granny's past-their-best loom weights and old mammoth tooth necklaces with bits missing!

The reasons that we keep things are as numerous as the boxes in a hoarder's basement. The most common ones are feelings of;

scarcity (*"I won't throw that away in case it comes in handy one day"*)

indecisiveness (*"I'm not sure I want to throw that away in case I regret it, so I'll just keep it"*)

guilt (*"My mom gave me that and even though I've never liked it, I'd better keep it in case she finds out and gets upset"*)

sentimental attachment (*"I can't throw away my kids' school books, even though they have told me to!"*) or

emotional reassurance (*"I feel comforted and reassured when I am surrounded by my collection of tiny teapots and Princess Di memorabilia".*)

Clutter in your mind is characterized by jumbled thoughts and incessant negative self-talk. You can't differentiate between the trivial and the important, everything is given equal weight. You think about the past, fret about the future, regret decisions you have taken and worry about ones you haven't taken yet.

This mental clutter comes from our own thoughts, but it also comes from external sources. As the Digital Age has come into its own, we have become subjected to an endless stream of data. A study by the University of California indicates that every day people are inundated with 34 gigabytes of information, equivalent to about 105,000 words, plus pictures, videos and games. The average American spends over 10 hours a day looking at a screen of some form or other, (*smartphone, laptop, tv, radio, DVD, video games*), with our children close behind at six and a half hours and growing. Although we don't absorb all this information, in the average American's life, it is there, everywhere, all the time. Small wonder our minds feel like dusty attics stuffed full of cobweb-covered boxes of thoughts and ideas.

When thinking about clutter, people often forget about digital clutter. Emails, crammed calendars, old files, downloaded games and films, e-books you have never read ... just because it isn't physically taking up space in your house does not mean it isn't harmful.
You may think that clutter is a fact of life and that it may not be that bad. After all, how can possessions, ideas or information in our physical, mental or virtual space have an effect, unless we allow them to?

Physical clutter can be a health danger, the dust and dander it collects are not good for people with allergies or asthma, for example. In extreme cases, it can lead to accidents *(some people have literally died after being crushed by their possessions)* and can be a fire hazard. Clutter can cause us to feel guilty or embarrassed that we haven't dealt with it, or frustrated as we fail to locate our keys or the latest bill from the insurance company under a pile of stuff. It makes us feel psychologically hemmed in and overwhelmed, constantly sending our minds the message that there is work to do and we haven't done it. It is also a constant sensory distraction, we see it, we may smell it, we touch it as we move it around or out of the way. It should be obvious by now, clutter is not a relaxing thing to deal with.

A 2016 study by Catherine Roster and colleagues at the University of New Mexico showed that many people identify very strongly with their homes and tend to be unhappy when they feel their home environment is overcrowded. The authors conclude that *"clutter ...can threaten to physically and psychologically entrap a person in dysfunctional home environments which contribute to personal distress and feelings of displacement and alienation."*

Clearing Clutter from Your Physical Space

Nineteenth-century English textile designer, poet and novelist William Morris said, *"Have nothing in your houses that you do not know to be useful or believe to be beautiful."* It is an excellent starting point when deciding to tackle clutter. Just think about his words for a moment and see if they make sense to you and if you feel you can divide all your possessions into these two categories.

Japanese tidying guru and New York Times bestselling author Marie Kondo has her own twist on this. She asks you to touch or hold each item and ask yourself *"does it bring me joy?"* It's such a simple little technique which may not work for household essentials like hammers and pliers (for those, revert to William Morris and his *"useful"* definition), but can certainly have effects far beyond simply tidying.

I have used Marie Kondo's method and can recommend it. If you have been avoiding clearing clutter then this makes it quite fun. First of all, forget tidying anything away. You can tidy once you have finished clearing clutter. Kondo recommends tackling clutter according to the type of object rather than room by room or drawer by drawer. In her opinion, clearing clutter is not something you should be returning to over and over again. Once should be enough and then you monitor everything else on an ongoing basis. She also recommends not beginning the process (and it is a process that could take weeks or even months) with any possessions that you have an emotional attachment to. Her thinking is that as you become better at selecting items that bring you joy and getting rid of the rest, then you will become better prepared to tackle the things that are harder to throw away because of your strong emotional ties to them, such as gifts or inherited items.

If you are to deal with your clothes, then Kondo advises taking all your clothes from all over the house and putting them into a big pile on the floor. Then you go through them one by one and apply the *"joy"* question. If this seems like too big a task then you can subdivide a category, so "clothes" could be broken down into "underwear" or "socks," for example.

Having done this myself, I can assure you that it is pretty easy to feel the joy. You know as soon as you touch something if you love it or not. It is also very easy to know if something is useful, even if it doesn't bring you joy. The textbook you need for college, the vacuum cleaner, the bottle of bathroom cleaner – they don't make you happy but perhaps the results of using them might.

What about the items that you hold up and then hesitate about. According to Kondo, something brings you joy or it doesn't, you know immediately if it does and any uncertainty means it doesn't. Marie Kondo may be small in stature and softly spoken, but she is quite a tyrant when it comes to being ruthless about clutter. She recommends immediately discarding the item or giving it away. That can be harder than you think. Your mind will play all kinds of tricks, inventing any number of reasons why you shouldn't do this. Maybe you will regret getting rid of it. Maybe you will learn to love it. Maybe you haven't given it a proper chance, you weren't really concentrating when you looked at it the first time. Maybe you should keep it because your partner, kids, friends love it. And so the list of excuses goes on. Because that is what they are – excuses.

If you are struggling with some possessions, then give yourself a bit of a break and create a *"not sure"* pile. Live with the pile for a few days, then redo the exercise. Hold each item again and ask if it brings you joy. (Or is useful). You might find it easier to get rid of things the second time around. If not, then rinse and repeat. What you are left with, apart from the useful things, is a reduced number of possessions which all please you or make you smile. That is such a great feeling.

What I like about this method is that it is so personal. You will hear many clutter-clearing gurus tell you, for example, to get rid of all the books you have read and probably won't read again as they are just dust gatherers and you should have spaces on your bookshelves. I have always loved books, not just because of the knowledge they contain but also as beautiful objects in their own right. To me it seems nuts to throw away books just because I have read them. They may be clutter to some people, but not to me. Using the Kondo method, I can simply go through and see which books give me joy or are useful. That is a much better approach than throwing all those volumes out and having empty bookshelves. To me, empty bookshelves look sad.

Everyone has a level of clutter they feel is acceptable and this is not something to feel guilty about. Some people are very minimalist by nature, love clear surfaces and nothing on show. Others are maximalist and are happier surrounded by more things. It's an entirely subjective and personal choice and is absolutely fine, as long as all the items around you make you feel happy or have some function. That is the bottom line really.
Having your environment as you like it, clean and filled with the possessions you love will have an immensely positive effect on your mind and body, so choose a tiny, achievable category and get started now.

Clearing Clutter from Your Mental Space

Clearing physical clutter is straightforward even if it is sometimes not that easy. The process is obvious, you identify something, remove it and then there is more space.
When you clear mental clutter, you are not removing objects, you are removing invisible things. You can't pick

thoughts or fears up and you can't see when they are gone, so you need a different strategy to deal with them.

Think back to a time when you felt very calm, centered and relaxed. It may have been during a vacation or a happy period in your life. You may have been aware at the time that you were focusing on the moment and not worrying about the past or the future. That is the feeling that you want to have on a regular basis, when your mind is not stuffed full of anxiety and negative thoughts. That is why it is worth clearing the clutter from your mind.
You can't separate your mind from your body and one of the best things you can do to create a clearer and less cluttered mind is to take care of your health. That means eating well, getting plenty of sleep and taking regular exercise. Remember your triggers in the last chapter? You may have noted that you feel more anxious if you are hungry, so eat! If white wine makes you feel like crap and gives you a fuzzy head the next day, then stop drinking it. In other words, take care of the obvious physical stuff before you tackle the inner space.

Deep Breathing, Yawning and Stretching.
Mark Waldman, who teaches the Neuroleadership program at Loyola Maymount University is the author of 14 books and is one of the world's leading authorities on spirituality and the brain. Among the many brain exercises he advocates is this very simple 30-second one, to be done about three times an hour or whenever you have an important decision to make or are feeling stressed. Simply yawn widely and mindfully two or three times and then take a deep breath and do some slow stretches, like you do when you wake up in the morning. Yawning with intent has been shown to lower stress and anxiety and releases

neurochemicals and increases blood flow to the brain. Waldman says, *"It's hard to find another activity that so positively impacts so many functions of your brain."*

Repeat a Positive Values Word.
Another of Waldman's simple but highly effective techniques is to identify your own most important value and then use it to calm yourself and switch moods. To do this relax, breathe deeply and close your eyes. Ask yourself *"What is my deepest and most fundamental value?"* and then accept the first answer you get. As often as you can, particularly if you feel anxious or are being bombarded with negative thoughts, repeat this value word. (For example, it might be "love" or "peace" or "creativity".) To be effective you need to use positive words five to seven times more often than negative thoughts and worries, so every time you feel a depressing thought coming on, just repeat your word over and over. The brain can't handle two contradictory thoughts at the same time and the positive will override the negative.

Write Things Down.
If things are getting overwhelming, it can be very helpful to write them down. Seeing things on paper gets them out of your head and also gets them back in proportion. Look at your list of problems and worries and then think of your values word again. Watch as those problems shrink in size.

Make a Plan and Prioritize.
I love a plan! If I am feeling deluged by too many tasks, then I divide a piece of paper into four sections labeled: urgent and important, urgent and not important, important not urgent, not urgent and not important. Then I put all the tasks I have to do that day into the appropriate

section, breaking them down into achievable chunks. I start with urgent and important, then move to urgent and not important and so on. It helps me feel back in control.

Deep Work and Focus.
As a counter movement to the 21st-century disease known as multi-tasking, there is ***deep work***. Although the concept of deep work has been around for a long time, the term was coined by author and computer science professor Cal Newport in his book of the same name. Deep work means working with focus and no distractions on one cognitively demanding task. People who practice deep work switch off email, cell phones, and any other distractions and then concentrate intensely, for between one and four hours.

Build in Time to Daydream and Play.
It may seem contradictory, but Newport and Waldman both advocate taking time out to daydream and switch off. Our brain can achieve great leaps of creativity and problem-solving in this so-called down time. History is crammed full of stories of people who have made their greatest discoveries or had their best ideas while relaxing or daydreaming. Einstein used numerous thought experiments to play with theories of physics, the most famous being when he imagined he was traveling on a beam of light, an imaginary game which eventually led to his famous General Theory of Relativity. In a world where busyness is valued over playtime and inactivity, make a stand for doing nothing!

Do a Digital Detox.
Did you know that there are some luxury hotels now offering digital detox weekends? They will take away your

smartphone and laptop and then suggest itineraries which will help soften the blow of being deprived of these precious objects. They are even reintroducing board games! You don't need to go to a hotel or pay hundreds of dollars to do this, but you do need a bit of willpower to ditch your devices. Set a time limit and then watch with wonder as the world unfolds in all its glory and proves to you that you can be there without needing the selfie to prove it.

Create a Sanctuary.
Find a quiet spot and relax. Close your eyes and then create in your imagination a special sanctuary, a place you can feel safe. It can look be anywhere you wish – up a mountain, in a forest, by the ocean, in a penthouse, even in the sky - and be furnished in whatever way makes you happy. You can return to this place whenever you want, as often as you want, and you will always feel calm, safe and protected.

Meditate.
There are numerous articles, courses, and YouTube videos online about meditation, so Google them and find one that suits you, or see if there are any meditation classes near you. One thing is certain; it is very good for your brain and your health, it calms you down and relieves stress long term. A very simple meditation involves relaxing completely by stretching then relaxing each part of your body in turn, then focusing on breathing in for six seconds, hold for six seconds and breathe out for six seconds. The idea is to focus on your breathing and to be aware of the thoughts moving through your mind, but not dwell on them. Just doing this for a short time every day will reap benefits.

Listen to Music.
Not just any music. Baroque music like Bach or Handel, with 50 to 80 beats per minute, can help you access the calming alpha brainwave state. There are also soundtracks which use binaural beats available online. These are best listened to using headphones as they rely on each ear hearing a slightly different frequency, this creates the effect in the brain of a third sound, which is the difference between the two frequencies being played into the right and left ears. The brain will then produce brainwaves at the same rate of Hertz as the new sound. Binaural beats can help the brain enter different states, including deep relaxation.

Get Creative.
Make a cake, paint a picture, sculpt a fairy from modeling clay. It doesn't matter what you do, but try to get hands-on creative every day. Apart from the satisfaction of producing something that didn't exist until you brought it into being, getting creative is also very good at destressing and relaxing you. My husband relaxes by cooking amazing meals after work, and I relax by eating them!

Chapter 4 Takeaways

In this chapter we have looked at:

- How your physical and mental space reflect each other.

- The importance of having clear, clean space both in your environment and in your mind.

- What clutter is and why it doesn't help you.

- Techniques to help declutter your physical space, including choosing to keep only things that are useful or bring you joy.

- Techniques to help declutter your mental space.

We have discussed a lot about how the mind loves to dwell on the past or the future, causing you to feel guilt, regret or anxiety and worry. One of the most powerful ways to tackle this is to master the art of mindfulness. That's what we are going to look at in the next chapter.

Chapter 5 Mindfulness – This Changes Everything

"Begin at once to live, and count each separate day as a separate life."
Seneca

Mindfulness seems to be the buzzword of the moment, but what exactly does it mean? Basically, to practice mindfulness, you put all your attention and awareness on what is happening right now, in the present moment. You pay attention to your thoughts, feelings, physical sensations and sensory input and to what is going on in the world around you.
You may think that you are mindful all the time, but very few of us are. Unless you are using a chainsaw, walking a tightrope or doing other activities requiring concentration and attention, the chances are your mind is distracted, teeming with internal chatter and thoughts of the past or the future.

In the East, mindfulness has been an important part of many spiritual practices, particularly Buddhism and Yoga, for thousands of years. In the West, *Jon Kabat-Zinn* has been credited with bringing it mainstream relatively recently. He founded the Center for Mindfulness at the University of Massachusetts Medical School and created an eight-week Mindfulness-Based Stress Reduction Program and writes and lectures extensively on the subject. Other figures who have had an impact on western thinking include Eckhart Tolle who wrote the best-seller The Power of Now.

If you think about it, all we have is the present moment. We experience this in different, subjective ways. It can seem endless if we are bored or under stress, all too short if we are enjoying ourselves or saying goodbye to someone we love. We can miss the present moment completely if we are performing routine activities that result in us *"switching off"*. I'm sure all of us have experienced the sensation of arriving at work and not having the faintest idea how we got there. Obviously, we handled a car, navigated traffic and arrived safely. But the journey itself? A total blank.

We can miss things happening in the present moment for reasons other than routine or habit. In one of the best-known psychology experiments of recent years, conducted at Harvard University in 1999, people were asked to watch a video of a basketball match. There were two teams, one in white shirts and the other in black. The observers were asked to count how many passes the team in white shirts made. After the short video was played, the observers were asked if they had noticed anything unusual. This is because, during the game, a gorilla (*well, a guy in a gorilla suit*) had walked across the screen, faced the camera, thumped his chest and left, spending a total of nine seconds in view. The jaw-dropping result was that half the observers just didn't notice it! They were so distracted by their counting task that they just blanked the big hairy beastie. It's quite astonishing that we miss so much and equally surprising that half the time we have no idea that we have missed anything at all.

Why is mindfulness important? Does it really matter that much if we miss stuff, or allow our minds to dance back into the past or spin into the future? The answer seems to be yes, it does matter. Mindfulness has been shown scientifically to increase feelings of well-being, reduce anxiety and worry and improve sleep. It has a positive effect on both physical and mental health and people who consciously practice mindfulness are generally more content and able to form better relationships with others.

Simple Techniques for Everyday Mindfulness

Because of the nature of our lives these days, we need constant reminders to stay mindful. Here are a few suggestions for incorporating mindfulness into your day.

Mindfulness Bell
There are free apps and websites which will sound a beautiful ringing bell tone at regular intervals. This is great if you are doing computer work. Set the bell to ring two or three times an hour and when you hear it, even mid-sentence, take a break, yawn, stretch and focus for a minute or two on your body and how you are feeling. You can get up and walk around the room, or jog on the spot for 30 seconds, or give yourself a quick but gentle head massage. It brings you back into the present moment and also refreshes your body and brain. Try http://awakeningbell.org/ for an online version.

Highlight Your Senses
This is quite an interesting exercise to try and you can also use it if you can't sleep. Sit or lie comfortably and take a deep breath. For five minutes focus on only one of your senses. Let's use sight as an example. Pay acute attention to everything that you can see, notice detail, light, shade and pattern in things you normally don't give much thought to. Look at places you don't usually notice, like the

corner of the ceiling. Let your eyes follow a shape all the way around. Notice different shades of color and how the colors change according to the light on them or their position in the room. Bring all your focus to that one sense of sight, ignore the other four senses as much as possible. When the five minutes is up, then do the same for each of the other senses in turn. This is incredibly relaxing and may become one of your favorites!

Walk
Fresh air is very good for you and so is exercise, so going for a daily walk is already a great idea. Walking in nature is the ideal, but you can walk regularly wherever you are. Instead of walking along immersed in your thoughts and missing everything around you, walk with attention. Feel the ground under your feet and the way the muscles in your body are working. Feel the wind on your face. Smell the earthy goodness of the woods or the damp of the grass. Touch the plants as you pass, feeling the difference between ferny fronds and rough bark. If there are wild strawberries around, then taste a few, or taste the fresh air and the sweetness of the rain. Look around you. Really look. As poet William Henry Davies said, *"What is this life if, full of care, we have no time to stand and stare."*

Bathe with Intent
Your daily bath or shower is a great time to practice mindfulness. Rather than just racing through this routine, pay attention to what you are doing, seeing and feeling, smelling and touching. Imagine that you are washing away negativity and stress and starting the day fresh.

Eat with Attention
We are all guilty of bolting our food down, especially if we

are in a rush. In my case, I get quite annoyed with my body if I get hungry and just want to eat anything quickly to remove the hunger pangs and get on with what I was doing. *(Yes, I know, foodies are always horrified when I confess this!)* But eating with mindfulness can not only de-stress you, it can also help you lose weight. Whatever you are preparing and eating, give it your full attention. If you are making something, then imagine you are adding a generous portion of love to each ingredient. Watch how the flour floats down like a white cloud and how the golden yolks of the eggs change color as they mix with the sugar. I won't get too poetic about this, you get the message I'm sure.

When eating, savor every mouthful, chew and really taste what you are eating. There are five different tastes: salty, bitter, sour, sweet and umami (Japanese for "yummy") which is a kind of meaty taste usually produced by glutamates. (Who knew?) See if you can recognize them as you are eating. That's quite a fun one to try with kids too!

Scan Your Body
It's all too easy to ignore what your body is telling you when you are rushing around like a whirling dervish. Take a couple of minutes to mentally scan your body from your head to your toes and just note how each bit of you is feeling. You are not only looking for aches, pains and tension, but also feelings of relaxation or comfort too. If you find any sore points, then see if you can rub or massage them to feel better. Your body will appreciate it.

Do Nothing
We are so conditioned to fill every waking hour with busyness that we have forgotten how important it is to

just do nothing, even if it for just a minute or two. Sit and look out of the window, watch the birds flying and the leaves of the trees moving, if you are lucky enough to have that view. If not, watch the traffic below or the little insect on your windowsill. If you have any thoughts, then just accept them and let them go.

Ditch the Tech
Spend as long as you can without your smartphone, laptop or tablet, whether that is five minutes or five hours. Whenever we have a break the temptation for most of us is to check our phones or surf the net. Don't. Do one of the activities I've just listed instead.

A Key Principle To Change

Mindfulness is not only being aware of what is around us and what we are feeling physically and mentally. It also involves appreciating the good things in life and being grateful for the smallest blessings.

Most of us express gratitude when we get a gift, or someone does something nice for us. This may even extend to writing a thank you note or email or sending a card to show your appreciation. However, practicing gratitude in a mindful way means being thankful every day, or several times a day, without having a reason. It makes you actively look around you and value all the things in your life that you normally take for granted, like sunshine and rain, having a roof over your head, not living in a war zone, having clean water to drink and being able to read and write.

These may seem very simple, even banal, things to focus on, but positive psychology research has shown that grateful people sleep better and are healthier both physically and psychologically. Gratitude is a great stress buster too. In fact, a 2006 study in Behavior Research and Therapy conducted with Vietnam War veterans showed a lower rate of PTSD (*Post Traumatic Stress Disorder*) amongst those with higher levels of gratitude. Grateful people have increased feelings of well-being, peace and self-esteem and are less aggressive. In other words, they feel happier! They are also less likely to be materialistic and more likely to be social too. Oh, and in case you need more evidence, grateful people live longer!

A Positive Change

As a way to move your focus away from the things bothering you and onto more positive aspects of your life, try writing down things you are thankful for. A list, a journal, a letter to yourself. And here's the proof.

The Emmons Lab, under the direction of Dr. Robert Emmons, Professor of Psychology at the UC Davis, California is engaged in *"a long-term research project designed to research and disseminate a large body of scientific data on the nature of gratitude, its causes, and its potential consequences for human health and well-being."* They have published reams of research material to back up the positive effects of gratitude and are currently focusing on the development of gratitude in children.

Their researchers discovered that people keeping weekly *"gratitude journals"* took more regular exercise and generally felt more optimistic about what might be coming up in the next week than those who didn't. They were also more likely to have moved forward on the achievement of personal goals.

Keeping a gratitude journal or simply listing the things you are grateful for on a regular basis is simple, free and has proven scientific effects. It's kind of a no-brainer really. Try to get into the habit of listing the things you are grateful for every night before you go to sleep or as soon as you wake up in the morning. Why not give it a try now? Think of ten things that you are grateful for in your life.

Being grateful is even more effective if you write it down, so take a few minutes every day to write down what you are lucky to have in your life. Don't just repeat the same things every day either. Being innovative with your list makes you focus creatively on all the good there is in your life.

A Helping Hand On Your Journey

If you are an animal lover, then keeping a pet is an excellent way to de-stress. A South African study in 2003 conducted by the late Dr. Johannes Odendaal found that the simple act of petting a dog releases feel-good hormones like endorphins, oxytocin and norepinephrine. Dr. Odendaal concluded the same would happen if petting a cat. Endorphins are your body's natural opiates and relieve stress or pain.

Animals are taken into hospitals, old folks' homes and hospices for the same reason. Their presence helps comfort and relax patients, bringing a sense of calm and pleasure. Just being near a dog or cat lowers blood pressure. They don't just have to be dogs and cats. Other species, including alpacas and llamas, are trained as pet therapy animals too and the effect they have is incredibly positive and uplifting.

If you are stressed because you have too many things to take care of and too many people depending on you, then looking after a pet is probably not going to alleviate your problems. But that doesn't mean you have to forego the benefits of being with animals. A 2014 study from

Washington State University showed that working with horses significantly reduced the stress hormone cortisol in children. The students who participated in the research spent 90 minutes a week with horses, either riding, grooming or interacting with them. There was also a control group who did not have anything to do with the program. After three months, the cortisol level of the kids working with horses had dramatically reduced. Even if you are no longer an adolescent, this will work at any age. You don't have to own or look after a horse yourself, you can take riding lessons or even spend time with them and get a similar effect.

Why does spending time with animals help alleviate stress? Animals keep you in the moment. They take the focus off you and make you feel less lonely and more loved. They give you immediate feedback in terms of wanting to play or enjoying a cuddle. They live in the moment themselves and don't hide their feelings, if an animal is happy or upset, you know it. If you are responsible for an animal, as opposed to just visiting one, then you have to make the effort to get up every day, feed it exercise it and take care of it. It can give some depressed people a sense of purpose and a reason to keep going.

Some animals are particularly sensitive to people in a depressed state or with certain issues like ADHD or autism and will actively seek them out and attempt to bond. People with autism enjoy the physical communication they can have with therapy animals, particularly horses, and these interactions provide a bridge to more normal communication with people too.

Many well-known animal "whisperers", like Mexican dog expert Cesar Millan and Austrian horse specialist Klaus Hempfling, have added human communication and self-confidence coaching to their array of skills because they understand that so many lessons from the natural world can also be successfully applied to people.

You can learn therapeutic massage techniques, like **The Tellington Touch**, to use on your pet. This gentle and relaxing method is extremely simple to learn and it will benefit both of you. Your pet will love being massaged and you will love the destressing effect it has on you as your cortisol levels reduce and your happy-hormone levels zoom upwards!

De-Stressing

Pets can really help you to de-tress. Make time every day to consciously connect with your pet. Spend a few minutes petting, grooming or massaging your companion animal. Play with your pet! You will forget about your woes for a little while and have some fun and exercise.

Watch kittens, puppies or other young animals. If you don't have access to the real thing then watch some videos on YouTube. (Yes, this kind of digital entertainment I will allow!) There is a story that King Charles 1 of England asked for kittens to be brought to his cell so he could watch them playing the night before his execution to take his mind off things, so if it worked for him...

If you don't have a pet, then volunteer at the local shelter, or do some dog walking or pet fostering so you can still get regular contact with animals without the responsibility of owning one.

Sign your pet up to be a therapy animal. If they pass the test, (not all animals are suitable) then going with them to visit the elderly or ill will bring out the best in both of you. If you don't know how, then learn to ride. If you do know how then start riding again. You don't have to bring yourself up to Olympic dressage standard, just enough for a gentle hack through the countryside will do.

An important thing to mention here is that animals take you out of yourself. They stop you from getting too inward looking and self-focused. Not everyone is an animal person, but if you are and you don't have a pet at the moment, then do consider how much good it will do you. In case you are worried about who will look after it when you want a holiday or have to work away, don't forget there are several websites connecting pet lovers who want to travel with pet owners who want someone to look after their home and animals. It's usually a mutually beneficial arrangement that is free of charge. So now you don't have any excuses!

Chapter 5 Takeaways
In this chapter we have looked at:

- What mindfulness is and its origins

- Why mindfulness is important in tacking stress and anxiety

- Techniques to incorporate mindfulness into your everyday life

- The power of gratitude

- How animals can help with mindfulness

Earlier we discussed how watching animals play, and actually playing with them, is great fun and very beneficial. Fun is such an important part of tacking stress and anxiety that I thought it deserved a chapter all of its own. Get ready to laugh!

Chapter 6 – The Power of "Fun"

"The human race has only one really effective weapon, and that is laughter."
Mark Twain

When you are stressed, worried or anxious, probably the last thing on your mind is having a good laugh and yet that is one of the best things you could do. Now, I'm not claiming that chuckling away at your favorite sitcom is going to cure all your physical or mental issues, but scientific proof of the benefits of laughter is unequivocal and growing all the time.

Laughter, smiling and generally feeling happy all help suppress the stress hormones like cortisol and adrenaline and release the good ones like endorphins and serotonin. Being aware of the power of laughter is important, because it can lead you to deliberately incorporate lighter moments into your day. You can't plan for funny things to happen to you, but you can plan to watch a funny sitcom for an hour every evening to make yourself feel better.

Did you know that the physical act of smiling has some very positive physiological effects on your brain and that of other people? Apart from being contagious, because it stimulates one of the unconscious automatic response areas in the brain, smiling also makes other people view you in a more positive light. A 2011 study by a team at the Face Research Laboratory at the University of Aberdeen proved that men and women found images of people more attractive when they were smiling and making eye contact. We know from personal experience that interacting with a smiling person is a lot more pleasant than someone who looks upset or just plain angry. It's very hard to keep your face twisted into a frown or scowl if someone is openly smiling at you, because it seems nature has programmed us to reflect a smile back so both parties enjoy that surge of positive neurotransmitters. The important thing to remember is that you don't need to feel happy to smile, but smiling will tend to make you feel happier. It might sound odd to smile when you feel miserable or anxious, but once you view smiling as another tool in your anxiety toolkit, a specific anxiety-busting technique if you will, then you might feel differently about trying it.

Being negative and looking miserable is a habit and it's a good one to try and break, because it doesn't do you any good and it certainly doesn't do anyone around you any good either. If you have kids, then being a good role model and making a conscious effort to smile whenever you remember to not only makes you a nicer person to live with, it also teaches them by example. It doesn't turn you into a Pollyanna type or a naively optimistic person, it is simply choosing to smile rather than frown and laugh rather than complain.

A Daily Dose of Laughter

If smiling releases endorphins, serotonin and other good things, then imagine what laughter can do! There are so many health benefits from lowering blood pressure to boosting the immune system that it's worth taking laughter seriously.

Back in the 1960s journalist Norman Cousins was diagnosed with a fatal illness called Ankylosing Spondylitis. He tried various remedies, both conventional and alternative, but they had almost no effect on his mystifying condition. Finally, he decided to check himself out of hospital and follow his own treatment program of laughter therapy, spending his time watching TV shows like Candid Camera and comedy films. When he had his next check-up, doctors could find no trace of the disease. Cousins documented this in his 1979 book Anatomy of an Illness, which was later made into a movie. It triggered a lifelong interest in the effect of emotions on someone's biochemistry and he wrote many other books on illness and healing from the layman's perspective.

No-one is suggesting that laughter can cure serious illnesses like Ankylosing Spondylitis or cancer, but it can certainly help alleviate symptoms and counter depression and anxiety. Ten minutes of laughter can reduce stress by up to 70 percent.

There are different ways to ensure you get your daily dose. The first is to take an inventory of what really tickles your funny bone. Make a list of all the TV shows, comedians, jokes, books, cartoons and YouTube clips that have made you laugh out loud in the past, and keep the list handy. You can keep adding to it as you find new things. The point of the list is to take time every day to revisit at least one of the items on the list. I have to confess that **"Ultimate Dog Tease"** on YouTube cracks me up every single time. If you don't know it, then do a search on YouTube. You've got the right one if it mentions bacon and maple syrup. Some of my friends don't find it funny, you might not either. The point is, humor is very personal. It's your list and if it makes you laugh, then write it down.

When you are feeling very anxious or worried, you may not be able to laugh, even at the funniest videos or stories, which is where therapeutic laughter can play a role. Laughter Yoga was created in the mid-1990s by Indian medical doctor Madan Kataria and they encourage participants to *"laugh for no reason"*. to simulate laughter until the real thing kicks in. Apparently, it only takes ten minutes a day to feel a real difference. There are over 10,000 laughter yoga classes and clubs all over the world if you want to give it a go. You can type Internal Jogging (such a great title!) into YouTube to watch a short documentary about it.

You might like to try and find your own laughter role model. This could be a funny celebrity, a friend with a playful nature, or even someone like Scandinavian "Laughter Guru" Thomas Flindt, who teaches laughter to individuals and big business through workshops and yoga sessions. The companies that have participated have reported higher sales and profits since introducing the laughter therapy, plus of course their employees are happier. In his book Happy Lemons he writes: **"Breathing and laughing are your most important energy resources. It doesn't make you feel alive, it keeps you alive."**

If you are in the habit of keeping a journal or diary, and I thoroughly recommend that you do, then make sure you note the funny stuff that happens to you every day as well as the drama.

How To Share the Fun

Have you heard of *"random acts of kindness"?* Maybe you have also heard the term *"paying it forward"?* Both of them have the same basic concept at their core, that you do a good deed for someone either because someone has done one for you or just for the sake of it. If the random act of kindness is for a stranger and is anonymous, it's even better. Now why on earth would you want to pick up the tab for the old lady sitting in the corner of the coffee shop or pay the toll on the freeway for the person behind you?

The Random Acts of Kindness Foundation has research to show that there are many positive effects to being kind, and not just for the recipients of the good deed. They cite research from Emory University concerning the *"helper's high",* an effect brought on by being kind to another person, which activates the reward and pleasure centers in the giver's brain. They also report: *"Witnessing acts of kindness produces oxytocin, occasionally referred to as the 'love hormone' which aids in lowering blood pressure and improving our overall heart health. Oxytocin also increases our self-esteem and optimism, which is extra helpful when we're anxious or shy in a social situation."*

It takes effort to do nice things, particularly if you are feeling anxious and stressed, but view it as necessary and beneficial therapy, with the added bonus of making those around you feel good. Don't reserve the random acts for strangers either. Spread the love around family, friends and acquaintances and then wallow in all the positive changes you notice in your life.

While we are on the subject of spreading the love, let's consider social media for a moment. If your Facebook and Twitter accounts are anything like mine, there will be lots of memes, videos and viral posts forwarded by friends. Many people forward things that are basically just rants or criticisms and I make it my business to delete those immediately. Life is too short to share gloomy, negative posts, is it not? On the other hand, if I receive or find something inspirational and uplifting, funny or fascinating I will forward it to friends, in the hope of at least raising a smile and creating some positive mojo. It doesn't sound that important, but as I mentioned earlier, small habits can have a big impact on your life, so you need to be aware of them and change any that aren't doing you good.

In Praise of Praise

Criticism and carping are easy. Sarcasm and sniping are easy. Misery and moaning are easy too. But praise, well now, there's a thing. A few kind words of encouragement or appreciation can go a very long way. They have the power to make someone's day and change moods in a heartbeat. I know, it's a lot simpler to say nothing to the check-out clerk or the waitress, just look down and pay up. Engagement with other people is energy-draining, especially when you are not in the mood for it. But in the light of everything else I've been saying about these activities being therapeutic, think of doling out praise as an exercise which will help you with your anxiety. It will make you feel better and will most definitely have a positive impact on the recipient.

You can always find something nice to say to a person, so start making it a habit to give compliments. Someone may have a lovely smile, or a great color of nail polish, or an infectious laugh. So, tell them, without making it sound fake or like you are coming on to them. Be genuine in your praise and don't wait for a compliment in return. Praise and run!

The Key To "Play"

As we have already discussed, mindfulness is a very good strategy for dealing with anxiety. Really focusing with intent on the here-and-now calms the mind and relaxes the body. Laughing and smiling, particularly the therapeutic rather than the spontaneous kind, can really make us concentrate on the present moment and appreciate that now is all we have.

Playing is another good example of mindfulness in action, particularly if you focus on the experience for its own sake rather than having an end goal. Children and young animals have no problem at all in doing things for the sheer fun of it, yet as adults we tend to lose that joy. Playing seems silly, pointless and makes us feel awash with guilt. Shouldn't we be working? Aren't there a million chores on our to-do list? In fact, this attitude is completely mistaken. Play is good for you, it aids creativity, helps relieve stress and anxiety and improves brain function. It triggers the release of our old friends, endorphins and can even relieve pain temporarily. Are you convinced yet?

It doesn't really matter what type of play you engage in, although I would say there was a pretty strong case for avoiding anything electronic or digital. Have a go on the swings in the park, throw a frisbee for the dog, roll down a hill like you did when you were nine, do a jigsaw or hit a tennis ball around with a friend. The most important thing is that you have some guilt-free time getting totally absorbed in something fun. It isn't selfish, and it isn't stupid. Even if you have a list of tasks as long as your arm and a load of people relying on you, you can always find fifteen minutes for fun. Remember what they tell you on aircraft about putting on your own oxygen mask first, before helping anyone else? Well, play is like your oxygen mask, because if you don't take care of yourself first, you will be in no fit state to help others, will you?

Real Life Case Study

After doing her detailed inventory, Serena now had a fairly good idea of what triggered her anxiety. She was certainly a lot more reflective and tried to make time to check how she was feeling at intervals during the day. She began looking at the anxiety as a thing she could overcome, rather than letting herself be defined by it.

She sat down one day while Amelia was taking a nap and thought about how her life and her behavior had changed. Apart from the stress and worry, she felt sad, like there was something missing in her life. When she followed this thought a little more deeply, she realized that she couldn't remember the last time she had really laughed uncontrollably or taken some time out to have fun. At work she and her friends would have what they called "mad time out" where they would all stop what they were doing and throw a paper ball around the office. If you dropped it, you had to do a forfeit. She smiled as she remembered having to talk to the sales rep from head office while standing on one leg as her colleagues smirked and made faces in the background. *"You need some fun,"* she said to herself. It was raining, but since when had that stopped her? She pulled on her jacket and rubber boots, scooped Amelia up and put her in her stroller then went outside.

Feeling a little self-conscious at first, she began jumping into the puddles in the garden, making the biggest splash she could. Then she stood in quite a big puddle and stamped her feet quickly up and down like a three-year-old. She found she was smiling at herself and she wasn't the only one. Amelia had woken up and was looking at her in amazement as was her neighbor Mrs. Harris. She waved up at her and then took Amelia for a walk, making sure she splashed wildly in each puddle on the way.

After her walk, Serena tackled some ironing while watching some episodes of **Friends** instead of the 24-hour rolling news show she usually had on. She'd forgotten how much she enjoyed it, she even found herself laughing out loud a couple of times.

She was surprised at how these two small actions lifted her mood, even temporarily. It seemed that laughter was the best medicine after all and the added bonus, given her precarious financial state, was that it didn't cost anything either.

Chapter 6 Take-aways

In this chapter we have looked at:

- The physiological effects of smiling and laughter

- The effects of smiling on others

- Norman Cousins, the man who cured himself with laughter

- How to plan a daily dose of laughter

- Therapeutic laughter and Laughter Yoga

- Random acts of kindness and paying it forward

- The power of play

When you are feeling stressed and anxious, you can often neglect your health and appearance, but looking after your body properly can help relieve some of the symptoms of stress, as you are about to find out.

Chapter 7 – How To Look After Your Body

"To keep the body in good health is a duty ... otherwise we shall not be able to keep our minds strong and clear."
Buddha

There is a strong and well-understood connection between the body and the mind, it is common sense that what affects one affects the other and yet so many times we treat them as two separate entities. We run to doctors for medicines to help us with a digestive problem or to help us sleep, focusing on the symptoms individually and expecting pills to make us better. Yet if we don't address the cause, if we don't use joined up thinking to realize that a dry mouth, aching muscles, high blood pressure, insomnia and stomach cramps could all be connected to stress, and that the cause of the stress needs to be tackled to alleviate the other symptoms, we will never truly achieve good health.

Your body is your friend. It is a finely-tuned mirror reflecting your current state of well-being, both mental and physical. Its natural state is always towards balance and health and the way it leaps into action when, for example, you get an infection or cut yourself is testament to the fact it is always ready to protect you and heal you. But if you abuse it, and by that I don't just mean in the traditional sense of drinking too much and taking hard drugs, but in a more chronic and insidious way, by regularly pumping it full of stress chemicals, not taking exercise and not eating well, it will find it increasingly difficult to do its job.

Tuning In

Do you know what worry feels like? Have you ever paid attention to what is happening in your body from the soles of your feet to the crown of your head? Don't worry, if you have never tried this then you are not alone!

Most of us pay scant attention to the micro messages our bodies send us all the time. Yes, when we get a cold, headache or a stomach upset then we take notice, but only enough to take something to make it go away. It's irritating when flu stops us from getting on with things, or a cough wakes us in the night, but apart from when things go wrong, we rarely check to see how we feel. We don't tune in, but if we did, it might make all the difference.

One of the most fundamental things you can do for your health, both physical and psychological, is to get to know your own body and how you react to both pleasant and unpleasant situations. So, let's try an experiment and see if we can begin to learn just how much information our body gives us all the time. The first part is quite unusual, in that you are going to think of something negative, but this is just to give you a benchmark. As you know, the brain doesn't distinguish between real and imagined events, which is why injured professional sports performers are often told to imagine they are doing their sport, as this *"mental work out"* has been proven to aid recovery almost as much as actual physiotherapy.

First of all, get comfortable and relaxed. Make sure you are somewhere where you won't be disturbed for about 15 minutes or so. Switch off your phone and other devices.

Close your eyes and start breathing deeply and regularly. It might help to breathe in for a count of four, hold for four and exhale for four.

Choose a situation, past, present or future, which you associate with worry and stress. Don't make this too traumatic. If you find it easier, you can think of a person who winds you up or who you strongly dislike. Try and immerse yourself in the thought, imagine you are there in the situation or with the person, see in your mind's eye what is around you and what you can hear and smell.

Now scan your body from head to toe (*or vice versa*). Notice how you feel.

Is there tension? Where is it located?
How is your breathing? *(Maybe you are holding your breath.)*
Is your mouth dry or full of saliva?
Do you feel nauseous or faint?
Really try to pay attention to your body.

Before you do the next part, use your imagination to create a good outcome to the scene you have just envisioned. If it's past, you can change history! If it's present or future, then make something nice happen. If it's a person you dislike, then imagine that they give you a present or a hug or apologize, or simply fade into the background. Close the scene on a positive note.
Now repeat the steps above, but this time put yourself in a positive situation or being with a person you really like or love.

How does your body feel now? Get used to acknowledging what a happy, relaxed feeling is like in your body. Do you feel it in a particular place? Your stomach? Your heart? There are no right or wrong answers, it's entirely personal.

Now slowly become aware of the room and your surroundings again and open your eyes. If necessary, make notes about what messages your body gave you in each situation.

Make a promise to yourself that you will tune in to your body, even if you have no symptoms, regularly during the day. Slowly, you will come to recognize how you react physically to both positive and negative situations. This can be especially useful if you have to make a decision with a few options and are not sure which one to take. Imagine the different options and pay attention to how your body reacts.

If you appreciate that certain emotions, thoughts and situations trigger physical symptoms of stress or anxiety in your body then you can take steps to deal with them. As we have already discussed, chronic stress does your body no good at all. The chemicals, like cortisol and adrenaline, that flood your system to deal with a flight-or-fight situation were designed to be short term fixes appropriate to a more primitive lifestyle, helping you to run faster or jump higher than the tiger that was chasing you. When the modern-day tiger is a traffic jam or a difficult boss and you can't hit them or run away then the stress chemicals are sloshing around with nowhere to go. The levels drop when the stress goes, but our 21st-century lifestyle means we have many stressors, so as the difficult boss walks away your computer crashes or the school calls to say your child needs to go home because they're sick ... and so it goes on. We remain in a semi-stressed state of alertness almost all the time and our bodies pay the price.

Unless we decide to adopt the lifestyle of a Trappist monk or a recluse, which may not be that realistic or practical, it is hard to remove the many causes of stress in our lives. But we can learn to take note of the warning signs and then take steps to deal with the situation. One good way of doing this is through movement.

Do This! This Can Change A Lot!

Don't worry if you are not very athletically inclined, because not all movement is strenuous. The point is that movement alleviates stress because it helps get the adrenaline and cortisol levels in your body back to normal.

Walking: One of the very best ways to get a movement "fix" is walking. It sounds such a cliché to say, *"take the stairs not the elevator",* but it is true, there are countless opportunities around to walk if you need them. However, in this instance we are talking about moving specifically to alleviate a stressful situation, rather than a regular regime (which is also an excellent idea, of course).

So, although you could run up and down the stairs a few times, and probably get a few funny looks while doing it, the best thing to do if you feel stress building in your body to simply go out for a walk. Research conducted at Stanford and Edinburgh, has shown that walking in natural surroundings is the most beneficial, even if this a park or botanical gardens and not the countryside. In Japan there is a tradition of Shinrin-yoku, translated as *"forest bathing"* and a 2011 Japanese government study showed that subjects who walked in the forest as opposed to an urban environment had lower levels of cortisol, blood pressure and pulse rate.

When you are walking to calm yourself after a stressful situation then try not to play it over and over in your mind. As we have already seen, the brain does not distinguish between real and imagined situations and you'll just end up even more stressed! Better to try a meditative technique as you walk, such as counting your steps, or a mindfulness technique as described earlier, like really focusing on the sights, sounds and smells around you and how your body feels as you are walking.

Sex: Jumping between the sheets when you have had a stressful time is another and perhaps more appealing way to feel better. Touching and hugging your partner as well as orgasm itself has been shown to release oxytocin which is the feel-good hormone that helps to lower cortisol. There are plenty of other anti-stress benefits that sex provides, including better sleep *(thanks to the post orgasm release of the hormone prolactin),* a good pelvic floor workout for the ladies, lower blood pressure and higher levels of certain antibodies, meaning you get sick less often.

Yoga: Practicing yoga is a great way to relieve stress. If there aren't classes near you or you don't have the time or inclination to go to an organized session, then you can easily follow along with guided classes on YouTube. Apart from the general health and relaxation benefits that yoga provides, there are specific poses that are designed to be almost instant tension, stress and anxiety busters. One of these, called Vajrasana if you are interested, is very simple and very effective, so follow along!

Kneel on the ground and then sit back down on your heels. Keep your spine straight and imagine a cord running through your core and attached to the sky. Cross your arms over your chest and tuck your hands under each armpit, leaving the thumbs out and resting on the area next to your armpit. It should feel like you are almost hugging yourself. Breathe in and out with long slow breaths at least ten times.

Swimming: This is another aerobic exercise which is good at helping relieve anxiety and stress. The movements in the water helps bring the fight or flight levels down to normal, a brisk swim releases endorphins and provides a good physical workout, the rhythmic breathing and regular, repetitive movements bring on an almost hypnotic or meditative state highly conducive to relaxation. The warm water itself (assuming you don't dive into the icy waters of a frozen lake or winter ocean) can provide a feeling of safety and almost womb-like tranquility as you float blissfully around the pool.

An article in Swimmer magazine entitled Staying Happy? by Jim Thornton quotes Aimee C. Kimball, director of mental training at the Center for Sports Medicine at the University of Pittsburg Medical Center who says, *"we know ... that vigorous exercise like swimming can significantly decrease both anxiety and depression."* While Moby Coquillard, a swimmer and psychotherapist from San Mateo, California says in the same article: *"I absolutely believe swimming can serve as a kind of medicine. For me, it represents a potent adjunct to antidepressant medications and, for some patients, it's something you can take in lieu of pills."*

Running: Like swimming, running is an aerobic exercise that helps with anxiety and brings stress chemical levels in the body back to normal. It also helps with breathing, and controlling your breathing is a very important technique when learning to control anxiety and cope with panic attacks. You need to build up to running, but once you do, the beneficial effects of a good, hard run can alleviate symptoms of anxiety for hours.

Tai Chi and Qigong: These Chinese exercise systems, both derived from martial arts, are perfect for relieving stress, their soft, slow, flowing movements and regulated breathing are like doing moving meditations, as long as you don't obsess about form and instead concentrate on breathing and relaxing. As with yoga, you can join a class or find some of the free ones on YouTube. One simple exercise is the great Tai Chi Circle. Stand with your weight equally spread between your two feet and your arms loosely down by your sides. Then while breathing in, lift up your arms and draw a big circle (one side of the circle per arm). When you reach the point above your head stop and while breathing out bring your arms straight down together in front of you. It takes about 30 seconds and is highly effective.

Breathing: This Is How You Should Do It To Reduce Anxiety

When you are stressed and anxious or having a panic attack, your breathing alters. You tend to breathe from the upper chest and often feel as if you can't get enough air. Because you are taking short, shallow breaths using your chest and not your diaphragm it can lead to a tight feeling as your chest muscles tense up. This kind of breathing also makes you feel nauseous and light-headed and can make your heart beat faster and cause your hands and feet to go numb or get pins and needles. Feeling you can't breathe is scary in itself, but add the other symptoms caused by over-breathing and it is no wonder you may think you are having a heart attack and panic. The advice is usually to take deep breaths, but this can make things worse unless you do them properly.

Here are two exercises which will help you:

Breathing from your stomach: Put one hand on your chest and the other on your stomach, around your beltline. Sigh and close your mouth. Then push your stomach out which will make you inhale through your nose. Pause and then open your mouth and exhale slowly by pulling your stomach in. Repeat, all the time breathing slowly and steadily and checking you don't feel dizzy or light-headed.

The Buteyko Method: This method of breathing is quite different from the first, but try it to see if it benefits you. It was developed in the 1950s by Russian scientist Konstantin Buteyko and involves breathing *"lightly, superficially and only through the nose."* Buteyko feels that many people breathe too deeply causing them to take in too much oxygen and over dilute the amount of carbon dioxide in the blood. There are exercises online that you can watch and try for yourself, just Google *"Buteyko breathing"* or type it into YouTube. The general principal is to train yourself to only breathe through your nose and to dramatically reduce the number of breaths you take per minute. It is also said to help asthma sufferers, not just those with anxiety.

Getting Better Sleep!

Shakespeare got it right when he wrote *that "sleep knits up the ravell'd sleeve of care."* A good night's sleep has numerous health benefits, in fact, it is one of the most important things you can do for your mental and physical health. Poor sleep is linked to a variety of conditions, including inflammatory bowel disease, decreased immune function, blood sugar issues, increased risk of heart disease and stroke, lack of concentration, and reduced productivity. Ninety percent of people with depression report problems with sleep and 70 percent of those with stress and anxiety problems say they have trouble sleeping.

The ideal is eight hours, but for many this will just seem impossible. One of the most annoying things about having anxiety and worry is that it affects your sleep, making you wake up in the night or have trouble getting to sleep at all. Lack of sleep then makes you feel terrible, but no matter how tired you are you can't sleep and then you worry about not sleeping - and so the vicious circle is set.

There are ways that you can optimize your chances of getting a good night's sleep:

- Eat the right *"sleep-inducing"* foods. These will often include tryptophan, melatonin or magnesium, all of which help induce sleep, or chemicals such as calcium, which help in their absorption or production. Foods include: turkey, walnuts, pistachio nuts, cherry juice, honey, kale, shrimp, banana, Marmite and hummus.

- Have a sleep routine, this trains your mind to expect to go to bed and go to sleep after following certain rituals, for example having a bath, having a milky drink then going to bed at 10.30.

- Don't have any electronic devices in the bedroom. TVs, smart phones, laptop, tablet – all a big no as far as sleep is concerned.

- Try bathing in a bath with Epsom Salts or massaging your stomach with magnesium oil as both contain magnesium, a very good sleep-inducer.

- Don't eat a meal or drink alcohol for a few hours before sleeping.

- Try herbal tablets such as valerian (an ancient sleep remedy) or tablets with melatonin in them.

- Keep your bedroom dark and cool. (Cool in the temperature sense, that is!)

+ Make sure you are physically tired, so try to go outdoors, exercise or have a long walk during the day.

- Don't *"saw sawdust"*. Leave the day's troubles behind you, imagine throwing them in the bin or having them written on a sheet of paper and turning the paper over. The point is, the day is over, and you don't want to spend the night reliving things you can do nothing about.

- Investigate some of the very good sleep hypnosis or guided meditation videos on YouTube. Plug in your earphones, close your eyes and you'll be asleep before you know it.

Looking After Yourself

You must learn to be your own best friend and fiercest advocate, therefore you need to have some little treats which needn't cost the earth but can make you feel pampered and spoilt. One common symptom of depression is self-neglect, but it's amazing how much of a boost something as simple as wearing a different color or having a new hairstyle can be. These little treats needn't cost the earth or be complicated either. A nice soak in the bath with some bath oil or bubble bath is relaxing and indulgent without being expensive. Listening to your favorite music, watching a good movie, buying yourself some flowers or a lovely box of chocolates or treating yourself to a magazine or a good book are great ways to spoil yourself too. Remember, it's a personal thing, you know best what makes you feel good. Have some fun and make a list of your top ten treats, then make an effort, even if you don't feel like it, to incorporate at least one treat into every day.

Of course, if you want to push the boat out a bit then a massage or spa treatment or a makeover can really make you feel special. And you can look after your body in a different way by planning a lovely meal in your favorite restaurant or buy a bottle of your favorite wine. The point is, it should move you from the mundane to the extraordinary, it should lift your spirits and make you smile. And why not? You deserve it!

Chapter 7 Takeaways

In this chapter we have looked at:

- The mind/body connection

- How to tune into your body in both positive and negative situations

- Different ways to destress using movement and exercise

- The importance of how you breathe and two breathing techniques

- The power of sleep and different ways to ensure you get your full quota

- Some important ways to pamper yourself

In the next chapter we are going to look at the other vital aspect of your own wellbeing, your mind and how you can best use it to conquer anxiety and worry. So, let's find out more!

Chapter 8 – Easily Harnessing The Power of your Mind

"The energy of the mind is the essence of life."
Aristotle

Your mind is the most powerful tool you possess. It governs everything, how you perceive and process information, how you react to things, what you feel, what you think. It is the source of your imagination, your creativity and your dreams. Even your five senses are processed in your mind. Your nose may be the thing that does the sniffing but it's your mind that decodes the smell!

Deciding to learn more about your how your mind works and to take control of your thoughts is one of the most important things you can ever do, a gift to yourself. Yet the vast majority of people will never bother to do this and will spend most of their lives *"asleep",* not aware of just what they could achieve if they decided to master their thinking.

So, first of all, you should congratulate yourself on being interested enough to get this far. You are already in the minority. You already have a huge advantage over most people. The mind is truly incredible and the more you learn about it, the more you will appreciate just how it can help you not only overcome anxiety and worry, but also give you the confidence to build the life you deserve.

Here are a few facts about the mind that may surprise you and, I hope, fill you with appreciation for the powerhouse between your ears.

- According to latest estimates we have 86 billion brain cells.

- We each have about 50,000 thoughts per day. However, it's been estimated about 70 percent of this mind talk is negative! *(Self-criticism, anxiety and so on.)*

- There are about 400 miles of blood vessels in the brain.

- Your brain can change and develop new cells throughout your lifetime.

- The memory capacity of the brain is 1015 bytes - the same as the whole World Wide Web.

- The human brain is 30 times more powerful than some of the world's fastest supercomputers.

- About 95 percent of decisions happen in your subconscious mind.

- You have "secondary brains" in your intestines (100 million neurons) and your heart (about 40,000 neurons), which throws light on the expression "gut feeling" and may also explain why many heart transplant subjects take on the memory and personality of their donors.

There are many, many more facts about your brain than those, and if you are interested you can research it in Google. But what I hope you get from this is just how complex and truly incredible the mind is, yet we are never taught how to use it properly. I certainly never had a *"user's manual"* when I was in school.

You Are What You Think

The mind can be your best friend, but it can be your worst enemy too. Shakespeare put it very well when he wrote: *"There is nothing either good or bad, but thinking makes it so."* The poet John Milton echoed this when he wrote: *"The mind is its own place and in itself can make a Heaven of Hell, a Hell of Heaven."*

The mind plays a big role in stress or worry, and you can literally think yourself into, and out of, a panic state. This is not to apportion blame. Don't feel that your anxiety is a figment of your imagination. The fears and symptoms are very real, and it is not your fault if you feel this way. The important thing now is to understand the role of the mind in anxiety and stress, and help harness its power in a positive way to help you feel better.

If you have heard the expression a *"self-fulfilling prophecy"* then you will know that people very often get what they expect, good or bad. I have a friend who is very loyal and kind to her family and close friends, but thinks strangers are out to cheat her and can't be trusted. She believes that *"you should kick dirt in people's faces before they kick dirt in yours."* Of course, this isn't true, but she approaches every transaction with this attitude and treats people in an aggressive and distrustful way that doesn't bring out the best in those she is dealing with. They can feel her hostility and dislike and are therefore defensive in their responses. The result is that everything gets off on the wrong foot and often degenerates from there, which leads her to say,

"You see, I told you they couldn't be trusted!"

Research has discovered that we use the same part of the brain to think about the past and the future. That's why we tend to anticipate the outcome of future events based on past experience. If you lost your way when driving in a new place then you will understandably feel anxious that the same thing will happen again next time you drive somewhere you aren't familiar with. The degree of anxiety will reflect what happened in the past, so if you once got lost in a snowstorm at night then this will have more of an impact than making a wrong turn on a spring day.

Add to this the fact that your mind loves having *"little chats"* with you, often fear-inducing or negative, and you can see how a scenario could build up*: "Oh, so you have to drive to Fairfield for the job interview? Well you don't know where that is, do you? We all know how great you are at directions, so you're bound to get lost. It'll be like West Hampton all over again! Weather looks bad too, it'll probably snow or rain, knowing your luck. It's going to take hours to get there too, especially if you take a wrong turning, which you will, so it'll be dark. You know how bad you are at driving in the dark. Actually, you're pretty bad at driving, period, aren't you? Probably best not to go. You won't get the job anyway. Remember the last time? ..."*

Sound familiar? We all do this to some extent, but if you suffer from anxiety, you do it more than most. The good news is that there are ways to counter it. Awareness is key. Understanding what is going on and why your mind is doing this is half the battle. You may not be able to stop the memories of a negative situation or the stream of chatter in your head, but you can choose not to react to it.

Taking Control

Mastering your thoughts and your inner chatter is an ongoing process and you need to check in a lot to make sure you are on top of things. The steps you take are not that hard, but as the saying goes: *"it's simple, but it's not easy"*.

Your mind is constantly at work. A lot of what it does is to screen information so that you don't get overwhelmed with the millions of messages your brain takes in every day. It sorts out the relevant from the inconsequential and draws things to your attention that you have indicated are important. This may be something you have been focusing on. For example, if you wanted to buy a blue dress for a wedding you then start seeing blue dresses everywhere. There aren't any more blue dresses than before, it's just that you have sent your brain the message that you are now interested in them, so what is called the reticular activation system no longer ignores them but highlights them for you instead.

That is all well and good for innocuous things like blue dresses, but if you constantly fret over negative things and reinforce them by focusing on them all the time, then your brain will still do its thing and bring examples to your attention because it thinks that they are important to you. A friend of mine Robin lives in California. She is constantly thinking about earthquakes. Now, residents of California know that there are sensible precautions to take when you live in an earthquake zone: knowing the safest spot in a building, having an emergency bag packed and so on, but Robin takes this a lot further. She follows stories about earthquakes from anywhere in the world in the news and social media *(there's always an earthquake happening somewhere)* and regularly visits an earthquake reporting website. She won't put any pictures up in her rented apartment in case they get damaged when they fall off the walls when the earthquake hits.

She is a little bit obsessed by earthquakes and because she spends such a lot of time thinking about them, her brain has made the understandable assumption that earthquakes are important to her and so flags up lots of earthquake-related things all the time. I remember being with her at the airport and she dragged me half way across the shopping center to a bookstall where she had somehow, from many feet away, spotted a book about earthquakes on sale. I hadn't even noticed the bookstall! She lives her life in a constant state of anxiety and fuels her fears by feeding them.

This is an extreme example, but you get the point. You can turn your everyday life into a negative and pretty scary place if you constantly focus on the bad things about the world and about yourself. Fortunately, the opposite is also true. In his book **The Luck Factor: The Scientific Study of the Lucky Mind**, British psychologist Professor Richard Wiseman decided to make a scientific investigation of just what makes some people luckier than others. He placed ads in the press asking people to contact him if they thought they were extremely lucky or extremely unlucky. He then did a detailed analysis of the lives of the 400 volunteers from all walks of life who contacted him over the years. Some really did appear exceptionally lucky or unlucky. Wiseman asked them to write diaries, fill in questionnaires, be interviewed and take part in experiments. After all these years of research this is what he concluded: *"...lucky people generate their own good fortune via four basic principles. They are skilled at creating and noticing chance opportunities, make lucky decisions by listening to their intuition, create self-fulfilling prophesies via positive expectations, and adopt a resilient attitude that transforms bad luck into good."*

Wiseman's conclusions are very encouraging. He states that you can learn to be lucky. In fact, in the book he describes how he started a Luck School, training the self-confessed unlucky people how to attract greater good fortune with often startling results. What can we learn from this to help overcome anxiety and worry? Let's look at a few ideas from the book.

Shake things up a bit. Lucky people tend to deliberately break their routines and introduce variety. If they feel they are getting into a rut, then they will deliberately attempt to change their behavior. This makes sense because repeating familiar routines blinds you to them. You are far more likely to notice opportunities in unfamiliar surroundings because you are having to pay attention and be mindful of what's happening. In the same way, to stop hanging out with the same group of people, do something that will force you to meet new ones. Wiseman describes how one of the participants in the book decides only to talk to people wearing a particular color at a party, for example.

Thank your lucky stars. Not all of life is sunshine and roses, even lucky people have bad things happen to them. The trick is in how you deal with the crap! Rather than look at the glass half empty, try the opposite. If someone bumps into your car and makes a small dent in the door, then make an effort to be grateful it wasn't something more expensive and more serious, rather than focusing on how unlucky you were to be in the wrong place at the wrong time and why does this always happen to you? Yes, it takes practice to look at things this way, but it is worth it.

Dear Diary, Guess What Happened?: Every evening, write down all the lucky and positive things that have happened to you each day, no matter how small. Even if you found a cent on the ground, write it in your diary! Read the list from the previous day before adding today's events. As the list builds and you start appreciating the number of good things happening to you, you will begin to focus on that and not the bad.

There are some other techniques you can use to master your thoughts and feel less anxious. One of the most straightforward is to observe your own mind at work. Become aware of what you are thinking and just observe without judgement. The only requirement is to notice. You don't criticize, you just start paying attention to how that gray matter between your ears is working. Is it wandering? Is it focused? Is it regurgitating old worries and playing back long-gone scenarios? Watch your thoughts as they come and go.

If you really want to go really deep, then think about this. When you notice *"Ah, I'm feeling quite anxious at the moment and I'm thinking a lot about what might happen tonight,"* which part of you is noticing that? Which part of your mind is stepping back and observing? Interesting, huh?

Now imagine that you can enter into the space between thoughts, the space where that observer lives. What would that be like? Can you feel, even for a second, what it is like in that perfect and peaceful space? A space without thoughts? A space to just be? Even trying to do this for a short time, or thinking about this space, will create an awareness that you are not your thoughts. Your thoughts run through your mind, but they are not who you are.

The Steps To Reframing Your Thoughts

There is a way that you can change how you react to and interpret something negative that is happening or has happened to you. It's called reframing. Our negative thoughts are not helpful and it is worth learning how to recalibrate them in order to feel happier.

It should now be obvious that many of your thoughts are a product of your experience, beliefs and assumptions. Something happens, but that event in itself is neutral. It is only our interpretation of it that gives it significance. This is not in any way to downplay tragedy, but even there, good can come out of disaster. Different people can view the same situation and be affected in profoundly different ways, depending on the way they think, what they believe and their own life history. For example, a snowstorm causes one person to panic because she hates driving in snow but has to get to work, a child to clap their hands in excitement as they think about a day off school and building a snowman, the CEO of a salt company to smile at his increased profits as he sends out extra supplies to the highway companies and a young man to start crying as he remembers how his late Mom used to love the snow. You see how we can interpret things differently?

Once you are aware that events are in themselves neutral and that your thoughts are shaping your interpretation, even if this is to try and help or protect you, then you can try reframing them. Here is one way:

- Think of a situation that affects you in a negative way

- Try and work out how you are framing it. What is making you view it so negatively? Is it because of certain limiting beliefs you hold? A past experience? A set of beliefs that may not even be yours? Old fears and phobias?

- If the situation is a learning experience, what is it teaching you?

- What advice would you give to a friend looking at the situation in the same way?

- What kind of language are you using in your self-talk about this situation? Can you tone it down a bit? Instead of saying *"I really, really hate going to parties,"* could you say, *"parties are not my favorite way to spend time, but they can sometimes be fun."*

- Can you set yourself a bit of a challenge? If you find you are reacting to a situation based on old programming or conditioning, then how could you look at it differently. Instead of saying *"I'm wasting my life, I don't even know what job I want to do, I'm just a jack-of-all-trades-master-of-none..."* like your dad used to say to you, then why not challenge your assumptions and reframe your thoughts. Is what you are thinking true? Really? Is not wanting to focus on one thing as a career a bad thing?

Many of the world's geniuses, like Leonardo da Vinci, were multi-talented. Also, these days, people no longer have jobs for life. In the 21st century a *"portfolio career"* is common. You are very lucky to have the opportunity to try out some different things, hey, you could even combine your skills into a new and fascinating business that has never been done before. It's an incredible opportunity to make the most of your individuality and unique abilities.

There are many more ways to help you tame the incredible but sometimes unruly creature that is your mind, but just start with these ideas, even just one of them and you have already taken huge strides. Well done.

Chapter 8 Takeaways

In this chapter we have learned:

- How amazing your mind is and what astounding feats it is capable of

- How it can be a two-edged sword, making you fearful and anxious or positive and motivated

- That you use the same part of the brain to look at the past and the future

- That mastering your mind is an essential life skill

- Your mind will bring to your attention things you regularly focus on, whether blue dresses or earthquakes

- People can learn to make their own luck

- You can use various techniques, including reframing, to begin to manage your mind rather than have it manage you.

Next, we are going to look at one of the most exciting areas of all (see how you are already getting excited. And you don't even know what it is yet!) We are going to dive into the magic waters of creativity. Hold onto your hat!

Chapter 9 - Creativity Is Key

"Imagination is the beginning of creation. You imagine what you desire, you will what you imagine, and at last, you create what you will."
George Bernard Shaw

There are many ways to tackle anxiety and stress and we have looked at a few of them in this book. But a neglected area is creativity, because it's something people often associate with actors, artists, musicians and writers. They believe that you have to have an outstanding talent or a brilliant idea to practice creativity. That is so mistaken! Every one of us is creative, it is as much a part of us as breathing or eating, we just forget sometimes how to let it come through.

Creativity is very helpful with anxiety and stress. By placing your focus on something you are making or doing, your mind is taken away from problems and worry. Recent research has shown that doing something artistic reduces the level of cortisol in your body. Getting *"in the flow"*, that feeling of being completely absorbed in what you are doing so that you lose track of time, releases dopamine and serotonin. As we know by now, reducing the stress chemicals and increasing the feel-good ones is a positive thing. As if that wasn't enough, another set of research has linked creativity and longevity. Scientists studied the records of a group of 1000 people covering two decades and discovered the more creative ones lived longer.

Creativity Easily Explained

So, what exactly is creativity? Cambridge Dictionary defines it as *"the ability to produce original and unusual ideas or to make something new or imaginative."* I think that definition contains a key nugget: *"to make something new or imaginative."* My personal definition of creativity is to produce something by the end of the day that wasn't there at the beginning. It doesn't matter if it's coloring in, cake making or composing a song. The end result is a design, a donut or a ditty. In other words, something that didn't exist before you metaphorically, or literally, got your hands dirty!

People mix up creativity and ability. There is a common misconception that creative things have to be brilliant, that they could be sold for a king's ransom. This is nonsense. First of all, beauty is in the eye of the beholder. If you love it, that's good enough. If someone else loves it, terrific, but you are not doing this for other people, you're doing it for you. Secondly, unless you are an artist *(and I use the term in its widest sense)* by profession, you are not going to sell your work. In fact, you may not even show it to other people, although you can if you feel so inclined, because it's not about producing a piece that is good enough to make a living from or to be exhibited, it is about self-expression and the joy of the act itself. I repeat, you are doing this for you.

So many people have hang ups about their self-expression. *"Oh, I'm useless, I'm not at all creative. I can't draw to save my life."* There are many, many ways to be creative and it really doesn't matter if the way you express your personal creativity isn't on a particular list of traditional creative pursuits. Although we have looked at one definition, creativity doesn't have to follow a special format or tick boxes or be recognized by society. That's the whole point. It can be anything you want it to be. If, when you are out for a walk in the woods, you decide to make a heart shape on the ground from some pebbles, that is creative. If you arrange a few objects on a shelf in a way you find pleasing, that is creative. If you suddenly find a few words arranging themselves in your mind to make a funny rhyme, that is creative. If you dance around the room when you hear a favorite song, that is creative. And in case you are ready to catch me out by saying *"but a dance doesn't produce a new object by the end of the day, so it can't be creative,"* you are wrong!

A creative innovation can be ephemeral. A dance creates a pattern in space and time that wasn't there before. It shifts energy and moves molecules. Just because you can't hold a dance in your hand doesn't mean you haven't produced anything imaginative. Think about music. If you go to a live performance as each note is sung or played it disappears, but it was a creative act, even if you can't physically touch it. Are you convinced yet?

Some Easy Ways To Be More Creative

Don't feel constrained by a list, but I'm going to include one because I want to show that there are many, many ways to express your creativity and you may find something here that you did as a child and have forgotten about, or that you haven't tried but would quite like to have a go at. Feel free to dabble, doodle and dance! Add to the list if you want.

Writing – a poem, a diary entry, a story, a play, a song, your biography, your grandparents' biography, a new name for something, a joke. You can even think about the physical act of writing and try calligraphy. There are some truly inspirational calligraphers on Instagram and YouTube.

Art – painting, doodling, drawing, coloring in (some of those adult coloring books or apps are great), making collages or treasure maps, drawing a cartoon, sculpting a dragon or a daisy from clay or stone, painting stones (why not!), designing a tattoo, making a birthday card, icing a cake.

Music – singing, drumming, humming, playing the piano or penny whistle, whistling (even if out of tune), bell ringing, filling bottles with water and making a tune (I don't know if that even has a name! I expect it does.) Composing on the trombone or on your tablet (there are apps).

Crafts – weaving, knitting, crochet (all very cool at the moment, how our grannies would laugh!), origami, quilt-making, robot-making (why not!), woodworking, pottery, straw dolly making, macramé, felting, sculpting, lace making, putting a ship in a bottle, making jewelry, flower arranging, jam making, making a campfire or fashioning a shelter from branches and bracken. Building a box girder bridge or a castle from Lego, or for real!

Performing – reciting Shakespeare or your child's poem, playing charades or taking the lead in the local amateur dramatics group, improvising, doing magic tricks, telling jokes, dancing and gymnastics, performing a mime or being a film extra. Acting as if you were confident and worry-free. (I thought I would throw that in to see if you were paying attention!)

Interior and Exterior Design – painting a wall, papering a hall, moving furniture around, making a path or a secret garden, creating a focal point, learning Feng Shui, planning a vegetable patch, grouping all your ornaments into interesting patterns. Experimenting with crystals, playing with color and light and pattern inside and outside your home.

This Can Really Reduce Your Anxiety & Stress

One of the reasons for the list above was to start you thinking about the kinds of creative pursuits that interest you. Don't think of this as wasted time or energy. Deciding to pursue personal creativity is one of the most valuable and helpful things you can do to tackle your anxiety. Although we are approaching it in a light-hearted way, please take it seriously. You are a creative being and need to express it. No-one will judge you. And in case you think you are a rational, scientific and logical person who *"isn't creative"* because that is for hippies and Bohemians, think again.

Everyone, and I mean **everyone**, needs to exercise their imagination and stretch their creative muscles. Almost all the world's great discoveries were made by people playing around with ideas, theories and objects. Very often the big breakthroughs in science were made during *"down time"*. Don't feel you aren't creative – you just haven't found your special niche yet. Maybe you have to invent one of your own!

If you are feeling a bit uninspired, then think back to when you were a kid. What did you enjoy doing? What did you always want to do but weren't allowed to? What did you long to try but felt you weren't good enough? There's usually something there that will ring a bell.

Sometimes the creativity needs a little kick start, so have the materials ready. Often the thought of getting things out or preparing to be creative seems a bit onerous. So, buy, paper, pens, crayons, glue, wool, whatever you are drawn to. Keep them near to hand. Then just pick something up and play around. It's important not to feel pressured into being creative, it should be natural and fun. Don't feel you have to label it or justify it. If you fancy beachcombing then just do it! It doesn't matter if it's considered a traditionally creative pursuit or not. Follow your instinct!

Your subconscious will start making suggestions or bringing things to your attention once you decide to allow this back into your life.
You will be amazed how many resources there are online. There are free classes you can try, videos on YouTube, articles and magazines. There's never been an easier time to explore a variety of different hobbies on a sort of "suck it and see" basis. There are also lots of classes and groups offline, probably many in your local area. If you fancy giving one a try, then go along. Most of them will be more than happy to let you have a trial lesson or attend a session to see if you like it.

If you are really stuck for ideas, then you can decide to adopt a radical approach and try the first creative activity that you see that day. *(As long as it doesn't involve buying expensive equipment or joining a six-month long course.)* A friend of mine did this a few years ago and ended up in a woodcarving class making spoons! He loved it and has continued to *"whittle"* ever since. He says he would never have thought of working with wood before, and he only went along because it was literally the first *"creative hobby"* ad he saw that day on his way to work.

The Time For Change

If you are not used to doing something imaginative or creative on a regular basis then you will have to deliberately timetable it into your day. This may seem odd or self-indulgent or even impossible. If you are a busy mother with a million things to do, for example, then setting aside some personal time may seem like a pipe dream. But look at it like this. You are reading this book because you are struggling with anxiety. You want things to improve and to take back control of your life. At the moment, you might be operating on less than full energy. You will feel better and so will those around you if you look after yourself and your own needs and learn to relax and enjoy life again. If that means planning in a 15-minute creative space every day, then so be it. You need it.

It really doesn't have to take up a lot of time every day, the important thing is to make this a new habit. As things progress, you will find time stretches and that you move other things around, even drop other activities, so that you can spend more time just paddling around in this artistic pool. It won't take long for you to feel the benefit. But as a start, you must make that decision. *"I am going to do something creative every day."*

Be flexible in your thinking. You can do everyday chores in a creative way, it doesn't just have to be time devoted to a hobby. So, when you are cooking or cleaning or ironing, look at ways to turn that into an exercise of imagination and fun. Remember in the last chapter we learned that lucky people shook things up and avoided ruts and routine? Try doing the same with the chores you have to do. Use a different hand, start in a different place, look up some hacks on the Internet and see if they work ... even the mundane can become an adventure if you are determined enough.

An Added Bonus

If the craft you decide to follow involves making something, then an added bonus is that you may find you actually like the stuff you make and want to do something with it. That is not to place any pressure on you at all. This is not a push to start a business or rent a gallery. It is the process that is important, perhaps more important than the end result. But for some people, that end result may be something you are quite proud of. In that case, you may find some options open up for you.

You can give away what you make as highly original gifts for friends and family. You just can't beat homemade and hand crafted. Speaking from experience, your efforts will be especially appreciated by people who make things themselves as they understand how much effort has gone into creating something.

You may decide to wear or showcase your creations. It is extremely satisfying to get complimented on something that you have made yourself, both offline and online on Instagram, for example. It is a real achievement to have produced something from scratch and you can be rightly proud of what you have achieved.

If they are of good standard and seem to be desirable, then you may decide to sell your things on a craft site like *Etsy*. It could lead to a money-spinning sideline or even a change in career direction, who knows?

Wherever creativity takes you, it is an exciting journey and apart from the boost to your confidence and self- esteem, time spent this way is a good antidote for anxiety and worry.

Real Life Case Study

Serena was starting to feel that she could cope more with her anxiety. She was aware of her triggers and was building regular *"fun"* times into her daily routine. She hadn't splashed about in puddles again, but that one time had done the trick, she understood how making the effort to do certain things could have a positive impact on how she felt. She was watching a lot less news and a lot more comedy shows.

After reading about the positive effects of the creative process, Serena decided she wanted to add that to her daily routine. The trouble was, she had no idea what activity to pursue. She had never thought of herself as a particularly creative person. She could knit and crochet and sew, but didn't particularly enjoy them much, perhaps because she'd been forced to do them at school. Nope, it would have to be something else. She sat for a moment, pen in hand, ready to write a list. She had read through the list in this chapter, but nothing really rang any bells or pushed any of her buttons. She decided what was needed was some visualization work. She was convinced her subconscious could help and give her an indication of what to do. She waited until Amelia was asleep, then sat down in a comfortable position and did some regular deep breathing, in for a count of six, hold for a count of six, out for a count of six and then asked her intuition to show her an image of the best creative activity to benefit her the most at this stage in her life. Serena was surprised to get an image of a church window with all its beautiful colors.

Rather than try to analyze immediately what it meant, she allowed the visualization to continue and was shown a different window, again with luminous colors. She relaxed breathed deeply and allowed her awareness to come back into the room. She checked Amelia was still fine and sleeping peacefully and then sat and reflected on the two images that she had seen. She knew they were stained glass windows. Stained glass? Was that it? She frowned for a moment, something was ringing a bell. The local free newspaper? Was that it? She retrieved this week's copy from the garbage and slowly leafed through the pages. There she found what her subconscious had been alerting her to. A beginner's course on stained glass, enrolling this Friday.

To cut a long story short, Serena enrolled on the course. They allowed her to take Amelia with her and so over a few weeks she learned how to make a simple plant holder from stained glass. Although she had never done anything like it before and always associated stained glass with churches *(hence the visualization)* Serena discovered the wealth of possibilities open to her using this amazing medium. When she was working, piecing together the different colored glass and planning the design she found that her attention was completely absorbed and she forgot all about her anxiety for the entire time she was in the class and a couple of hours after that. The moment she held her first piece in her hands she felt the most tremendous sense of achievement and satisfaction. The *"not very creative"* person had shown a surprising affinity for this unusual craft.

Chapter 9 Take-aways
In this chapter we have looked at:

- How creativity helps with anxiety and stress

- What creativity actually is

- The fact that creativity does not have to earn money or be something you can hold in your hand

- Different ways to be creative

- How to discover your own creativity

- The importance of making time to get creative

- Some other benefits

- Serena's experience in the case study.

So far, we have examined how you can take things into your own hands and do some practical exercises to alleviate anxiety. In our final chapter we do the reverse and examine how handing things over to a *"Higher Power"* might be the answer. So let's see.

Chapter 10 - Handing Things Over

"All shall be well, and all manner of things shall be well."
Julian of Norwich

In this book you have been asked to take action, learn more, or make decisions about your anxiety. But this final chapter is different. We are going to consider the consequences of believing that you can hand over the problem to a *higher power*.

What you understand by higher power is very personal. According to some polls, around 80 percent of the world's population say religion or their faith plays an important part of their lives. Some scientists also believe that the human brain is *"hardwired"* for spiritual belief. But you don't have to practice a specific religion to believe that there is a powerful energy outside yourself. Whether you call it God, the Universe, Mother Earth, All That Is or even The Force, it doesn't really matter, that should be very clear. I am not advocating you must follow traditional religion here.

It can be tremendously reassuring to feel that something, or someone, bigger than ourselves is there to share the burden and listen to our problems. Sometimes it's so tiring trying to be strong and brave and positive that it's little wonder the saying *"let go and let a higher"* is such a popular one.

Let's look at that expression for a moment. Does believing in God or the Universe mean sitting back and doing nothing and simply hoping that someone else would just come in and take over? I would answer that by reminding you of the old joke.

A man is sitting on the roof of his house, surrounded by flood water. A neighbor rows by in a small boat. *"Get out while you can!"* he shouts. *"There's space in my boat."* The man waves him away.

"God will save me," he says. An inflatable lifeboat pulls up next. *"Jump in,"* they cry. *"No, don't worry,"* replies the man, *"God will save me."*

So, the lifeboat speeds away. Next comes a helicopter. *"We'll send a rope down, grab hold of it and we'll winch you up,"* they shout. *"I don't need a rope,"* shouts back the man. *"God is going to save me."* So, the helicopter flies off. The waters get higher and higher and finally the man screams *"God! I thought you would save me! Where are you?"* A booming voice replies: *"I sent your neighbor, a lifeboat and a helicopter, what more do you want me to do?"*

Very funny, isn't it? And as with all the best jokes, there's a lot of truth in it. When faced with a problem, you can't just sit back, do nothing and expect a higher power to swoop in and rescue you. You have to make some kind of effort yourself, you have to be aware of opportunities and solutions, because often they are all around you, if you just look. And help, when it comes, is not necessarily in the form you are expecting either. You have to be open to everything, not just what your preconceived ideas tell you. In other words, the higher power has your back, but expects you to do your bit too, at least that's my take on it.

It Can Help, If You Let It

Scientific research has shown that people with a spiritual or religious belief are less anxious and can cope better with stressful situations. The power of prayer is positive too. In a book by Larry Dossey called Prayer is Good Medicine he says: *"More than 130 controlled laboratory studies show, in general, that prayer or prayer like states of compassion, empathy and love can bring helpful changes in many types of living things, from humans to bacteria. This does not mean prayer always works, any more than drugs or surgery always works but that, statistically speaking, prayer is effective."*

An important caveat here is that you must never think your anxiety is caused by *"sin"*, failing to go to church, not believing in God or not following a religion. You should not feel guilty or think that this is some kind of punishment. Some religious practices can make you feel like this. If that is the case I would suggest that you keep going on your spiritual quest, but look for a path that is more positive and supportive. Also, there are no quick fixes and easy answers. A faith will not magically make you feel better. But having hope for the future and knowing you are being cared for and loved will make a difference in your life.

Deciding What You Need

These days it seems you can almost pick and mix spiritual traditions to find the best one to fit you. The Internet and social media have helped shape this, although it has its roots a few decades ago with the rise in popularity of the

New Age movement. But there is a downside to this. Too many options can be confusing, leading to paralysis of choice. It is a good thing, in any area of life, to drill down and focus, to go deep.

Although there is lots of information online, including quizzes to find out the form of spirituality that best fits you *(take a look at Beliefnet),* this is such an important issue that it is probably best to talk it through with a really good and impartial friend *(not one who is fixated on any one practice)* or a spiritual advisor. A good priest, for example, although they will inevitably want you to follow their own religious practice, should be able to give you honest and impartial advice about the options open to you, so if you know a spiritual advisor, even if not of your religion, then ask if you can have a chat. The point is that you need to talk to someone honest who will not be pushing a weird practice or cult or their own agenda.

There are different types of spiritual paths open to you, from simply being in nature and communing with the earth to yoga to a more conventional religion, like Christianity or Judaism, which may have within it various traditions from very liberal to more orthodox. It is a very personal thing, some people prefer to have more rules to follow and a very clear and organized system of worship, others prefer a freer approach. There is something out there which will speak to you, but if you find it then explore it deeply and seriously. Give it a chance to work, don't flit from one spiritual practice to another like a butterfly.

Exploring Alternatives

Deciding *"there must be more to life than this"* is a very common and important feeling. Many, many people are investigating different aspects of their own spirituality, because it is a fundamental part of being human. We crave this knowledge. Some can spend a lifetime seeking it.

It is important to say that the search itself is a valid and calming exercise. Reading books about different aspects of spirituality, watching videos, going to talks, chatting with friends - just learning more about something which is a part of everyday life and yet so different from our mundane day-to-day tasks is a wonderful and fulfilling way to spend your time.

It is often said that the spiritual path is like going on a spiral path up a mountain. You go round and round and end up in the same place, except that each time you are a bit higher up!

If you are feeling confused on your search, not sure if you should return to your own childhood faith, go New Age, become a Buddhist or a Druid, and you have tried the suggestions of talking to a trusted friend or spiritual advisor from a mainstream organization, then one thing that can help you is to access your own subconscious. We have talked about this before. Just as dreams can be an insight into how you are feeling about a situation or problem, so can some forms of guided visualization or meditation.

When asking your subconscious to help you, it is very important to phrase your question clearly. Sit down quietly and have a pen and paper to hand. Think about the issue you would like guidance about. In this case, a good question could be: Which spiritual discipline is best for me to help with my overall wellbeing and as an aid to anxiety?

If you are weighing up two or three options, then think clearly about what those options are and what you want to know. For example:
I am considering Wicca, Druidry and Celtic Christianity. Please show me which would help me most in terms of my wellbeing and peace of mind.

Once you are clear on your question, then you can try to get an answer. Here are three possible methods to experiment with. If you feel you need to then you can say a short prayer beforehand asking God or Spirit to guide you and protect you and to bring you the wisest answer for your good and the good of all concerned. Even though you are accessing your subconscious mind, it may make you feel better knowing you are protected. Another way of doing this is to imagine yourself inside a sphere of pure, white light which will protect you throughout the process.

Asking for Help

An alternative to going within and asking your Higher Self or subconscious for help, is to allow the environment around you to answer your question. This can be through a random event, a book falling off a shelf, a leaflet through your letterbox, overhearing a snatch of conversation, unexpectedly finding an unusual object or something else. If you choose to use this method then two things are important, apart from, as always, clearly stating the question you want guidance about.

Firstly, you must set a clear time limit, for example: the next three hours, by 8pm tonight, by tomorrow at 10am. Secondly, you mustn't try too hard. Don't look for a sign. The sign will appear and catch you by surprise. If you find you are seeing signs everywhere and struggling with what they might mean, then they aren't signs! A true sign is clear and unequivocal - and unexpected.

The search for something bigger than ourselves, something that gives us hope and reassurance, is one of the most worthwhile things we can ever undertake. It will help you with your anxiety and in addition, give you much more to enhance every aspect of your life.

Chapter 10 Takeaways

In this chapter we have looked at:

- How many people are on a spiritual search

- That you shouldn't just sit back and expect to be rescued, you need to take action

- How spirituality can help with anxiety

- How to find the right path for you

- The option of returning to your faith

- Different ways to explore alternatives

- Three ways to access inner guidance

- Getting an answer from your environment

Conclusion: Starting Again

"Your positive action combined with positive thinking results in success."
Shiv Khera

Well, we have a come a long way together, so thank you for reading this. I hope that the book has helped you in some way towards coping with your anxiety and stress. It is not pleasant to live life in a state of fear and you now know that there are steps you can take to help yourself. I hope you will try some of them.

If you find that your days are overwhelmingly dark and you can't see a way forward, I would encourage you to seek professional help. There is no shame in it and advice and exercises in a book like this can only go so far. For depressive illnesses you need more than I can give you and there is so much that can be done these days to help you cope and recover.

If you have approached this with an open mind and an open heart, then you will have learned some practical strategies to cope. You are not alone, remember. Whether it is a friend, a colleague, a family member, a spiritual advisor or a Higher Power – **you are never alone**. You are valuable and you are loved. Don't forget it.

I know you can do this. So, to quote our lovely Shakespeare for the final time, **"screw your courage to the sticking place"** and turn towards tomorrow with a warm glow in your heart. We're all rooting for you.

Good luck and here's to a bright and positive future filled with wonderful experiences and adventures.

Thank you so much for checking out my book.

I sincerely hope you got value from it. I hope it allows you to make important changes in your life. I hope this book helps you decrease your anxiety and increase your happiness.

If you liked this book could you possibly taking 60 seconds to write a quick review on Amazon?

Reviews are a vital way for books to get more exposure and help to spread the message. Anxiety and related conditions should be discussed, not ignored. Only through being open and spreading the word, can we help people.

Thank you. Your support is very much appreciated.

Michelle Galler

Printed in Great Britain
by Amazon